I0108270

Most people don't communicate well in personal and business situations. Without solid skills people flounder, time is wasted, and opportunities are lost. Decades of coaching, teaching, and observing have contributed to the substance of J. Robert Parkinson's *You Can't Push a String*. This book explores some of the problems and common misconceptions about interacting with others in business, social, and civic situations. Crammed with ideas and techniques that can be used immediately, the book is filled with personal stories about good and bad techniques and habits and highlights appropriate correct actions and reactions.

KUDOS for *You Can't Push a String*

In *You Can't Push a String* J. Robert Parkinson gives some no-nonsense advice on how to be both a better manager and a better speaker. He points out a lot of techniques that should be obvious, but aren't. He discusses things like how to write effective emails, how to deliver a clear and effective message, and basically how to get along with co-workers and make yourself understood. The book is packed full of good information you can use in both your personal and business communications. ~ *Taylor Jones, Reviewer*

You Can't Push a String by J. Robert Parkinson is a communications self-help book that is both informational and cleverly written. Parkinson covers most aspects of business and personal communications, as well as touching on effective management and selling techniques. Parkinson gives lots of case studies and anecdotes that are cute but make a point. He doesn't go into a lot of technical information, but instead focuses on common-sense techniques that you can put to use immediately. It's clear that Parkinson not only knows what he is talking about, but also that this isn't his first book. *You Can't Push a String* is full of good, useful information and is written in a light-hearted manner that is fresh and fun to *read.* ~ *Regan Murphy, Reviewer*

ACKNOWLEDGEMENTS

For years, many people have shared their insights, gifts, cares, and concerns with me on a wide variety of professional topics.

Their openness and willingness to contribute ideas and perceptions added greatly to the development and completion of this book.

There are too many to thank by name, but be assured I am grateful to each and every one of you.

I hope you find this collection worthy of your contributions.

YOU CAN'T
PUSH
A STRING

J. Robert Parkinson, Ph.D.

A Black Opal Books Publication

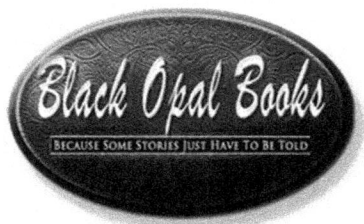

Black Opal Books

BECAUSE SOME STORIES JUST HAVE TO BE TOLD

GENRE: NON-FICTION/SELF-HELP

This book is a work of non-fiction. All information and opinions expressed herein are the views of the author. This publication is intended to provide accurate and authoritative information concerning the subject matter covered and is for informational purposes only. Neither the author nor the publisher is attempting to provide legal advice of any kind. All trademarks, service marks, registered trademarks, and registered service marks are the property of their respective owners and if used herein are for identification purposes only. The publisher does not have any control over or assume any responsibility for author or third-party websites or their contents.

YOU CAN'T PUSH A STRING
Copyright © 2014 by J. Robert Parkinson
Cover Design by J. Robert Parkinson
All cover art copyright © 2014
All Rights Reserved
Print ISBN: 978-1-626941-93-9

First Publication: OCTOBER 2014

All rights reserved under the International and Pan-American Copyright Conventions. No part of this book may be reproduced or transmitted in any form or by any means, electronic or mechanical, including photocopying, recording, or by any information storage and retrieval system, without permission in writing from the publisher.

WARNING: The unauthorized reproduction or distribution of this copyrighted work is illegal. Criminal copyright infringement, including infringement without monetary gain, is investigated by the FBI and is punishable by up to 5 years in federal prison and a fine of $250,000.

ABOUT THE PRINT VERSION: If you purchased a print version of this book without a cover, you should be aware that the book is stolen property. It was reported as "unsold and destroyed" to the publisher, and neither the author nor the publisher has received any payment for this "stripped book."

IF YOU FIND AN EBOOK OR PRINT VERSION OF THIS BOOK BEING SOLD OR SHARED ILLEGALLY, PLEASE REPORT IT TO: lpn@blackopalbooks.com

Published by Black Opal Books **http://www.blackopalbooks.com**

DEDICATION

To my wife, Eileen,

my first editor

and my greatest supporter

Table of Contents

PREFACE

A piece of string can be useful, powerful, helpful, and flexible, but only when it is pulled. It ties, tightens, and secures, but only if it is pulled. Because there is no rigidity, it is impossible to push a length of string.

In any situation where it is appropriate to provide guidance and direction to others it is essential to have a strategy and a plan of execution.

By definition, guiding and directing require a clear vision and a sense of direction. They also require key players to be out front, demonstrating and controlling the behaviors. It is impossible to lead effectively from behind other participants.

A piece of string is an excellent tool. It is flexible. It is available in a wide variety of strengths in order to match the requirements of a task. It is easily adjustable.

But it must be used to Pull, which means the user must lead the way.

Using a piece of string requires knowing two factors:

where one wants to go and where the starting point is. Without knowing those two points, it is impossible to set a course or design a travel plan successfully.

The intricacies of navigating communication vagaries, business interactions, customer attention, and a variety of interpersonal interactions require careful attention to detail as well as flexibility to adjust to changing personnel and situations.

Over time, I've identified material, examples, and anecdotes that address some of the more serious and the more common examples of options available in a variety of settings.

I have arranged these ideas into a dozen topic headings in this book which is a "think about…" book, not a "how to…" book.

The categories are loose and flexible, and it's quite possible a reader would include some of the material in categories other than the ones I selected. I won't stand toe-to-toe defending my choices, but I think, in general, they make sense.

This is designed for random reading so the sequencing is up to the reader. Start and end wherever you want and take whatever route is most comfortable.

The stories came from a wide variety of interviews, observations, and experiences. We all process and react to stimuli through our own set of mental filters so reader reaction could be vastly different from that described in each segment.

Use the stories as a work in progress. Review and evaluate the actions and examine how you might respond to the situations.

I hope you enjoy the read.

Introduction

In today's highly competitive market, every edge we acquire helps us succeed. The ability to communicate well with customers and co-workers is one of the sharpest of edges. If we tell our tale well, we can sell, motivate, inspire, and convince. Regardless of what we offer, someone else provides the same thing. There are few truly unique products or services – at least not for very long. Competition moves quickly.

All things being equal, people buy people, not things. That's why customers often follow employees when they move to new companies. They like, trust, and believe the people they have grown to know. We strive to build the relationships that are so important in every business, but precisely how do we go about doing that?

Our topics will include presentation skills, media techniques, effective writing, selling principles, handling difficult customers and colleagues, information security, e-mail, and voice mail to name just a few areas. Managing and Coaching will also be covered, as well as delegating and supervising.

I welcome this opportunity to share information I've gained during my years working in business, government, and academia. Here are some abbreviated segments to illustrate the focus and variety of the material.

Sell vs. Buy: Because salespeople know their product so well, there is a temptation to tell customers all about it. How it works. How it was developed. What it can do. Salespeople are good at that, but a sales interaction is not about "selling," it's about "buying." It's about determining what a customer needs and wants.

A ballpoint pen salesperson, for example, will not sell the pen if the customer wants something he or she can erase. Trying to sell a customer what he or she does not need wastes everyone's time and patience. That certainly isn't good for business.

The Presentation Data Dump: When designing and delivering a talk, many people simply say too much. And they often confuse and annoy an audience with a disorganized sequence. To avoid that, keep three words in mind: What? Why? How? Use that order to sequence a presentation, an e-mail, or a voice mail. What do you want? Why do you want it? How do you want it? That makes the point and gets results.

There's an old joke that states if someone asks you what time it is, just tell him. Don't' tell him how to build a wristwatch. Too much data hurts a presentation and will usually confuse – and sometimes anger – an audience.

Make your point, and move on.

Professional Manager vs. Non-Professional Manager: The professional manager asks questions and welcomes input, sees the staff as valued individuals rather than workers, teaches the staff to perform new tasks, delegates and enables them to take acceptable risks. The non-professional manager, on the other hand, often tells others what to do and how to do it, sees staff only as vehicles to accomplish a task, limits growth and development, expects obedience.

Other crucial business communication topics include: How do you get ready for a radio, TV, or print interview? How do you delegate effectively? How do you coach others to improve performance? How do you write a memo that is clear, concise, and complete?

This is just a brief overview of our business communication menu. There will be plenty of detail – but not so much detail that I violate my earlier comment about the data dump.

I look forward to building a strong and productive relationship with you. Please feel free to contact me with ideas, questions, objections, suggestions, and reactions.

Here's to the start of a long and productive relationship.

I can be reached at: jrp@jrparkinson.com

CHAPTER 1

Presentation Techniques

G et out front. Compel your audience to follow you. Pull them along – gently or forcefully – but do it. Don't expect them to willingly just tag along. They have plenty of other things to do. Make it worth their while to follow you.

Presentations consist of two major components: Content and Delivery. Most presenters concentrate on content and almost completely ignore the significance of how that content is packaged and delivered. In settings as varied as formal speeches and "elevator speeches," people in business, government, and academia, as well as civic and social groups, should recognize that the way material is presented often makes the difference between acceptance and rejection of ideas.

Presentations often become "data dumps." Audiences can't read visuals because the fonts are too small and presenters speak in a monotone so audience attention wanders.

Such presentations are just plain boring.

If a presenter isn't interesting, why should anyone be interested in what is being said?

In this section you'll find a wide range of circumstances and events where presenters were good – and why – and where presenters were bad – and why. Reviewing these techniques will be beneficial and productive, and that can change the impression audiences have of any speaker.

Audiences always remember good presentations. They always remember bad ones, too.

Dr. Martin Luther King, Jr.

I met Dr. King when he gave a speech in Stamford, Connecticut just a few weeks before he flew to Oslo, Norway to accept the Nobel Peace Prize. Many things about him struck me that night: –his humility, his warmth, his casual presence, and his ability to truly connect with his audience. His comments were both a preview of his acceptance speech and a review of the principles that formed the man.

I won't quote his words. We're all familiar with the ideas that drove his actions. But I will comment on his actions – that night – not during the entire Civil Rights Movement.

His words were powerful, crisp, clear, and carefully selected. That's why the content of his speeches had such a powerful impact.

What made him an effective leader, however, was his ability to package and deliver those words to inspire, to encourage, and to teach. It was his behavior, not just his words that had an impact on history.

Why was he so effective as a speaker? Why were audiences of diverse persuasions and backgrounds so captivated by him?

What were the techniques he used to support his words?

I won't attempt to provide a complete overview of his techniques, but rather to highlight a few behaviors all of us can use in our business relationships.

Let's look at both "Packaging" and "Delivery."

By definition, words are linear. One follows another so the order must be carefully constructed. Although it will seem obvious, many speakers fail to follow this simple 3-step sequence.

Begin. Develop. Conclude. Begin by making your "point." What do you want your listeners to know or to do?

Develop your idea by providing data, stories, illustrations, etc. which support, justify, and explain your point. Conclude by telling your listeners what will come next. What do you want them to do or to know when you're finished?

That's all pretty clear, but far too many speakers go around and around trying to develop ideas.

When listeners don't understand a presentation, it means the speaker didn't make his point. What a waste of everyone's time!

The Packaging we just covered is what you say. The Delivery is how you say it. Delivery includes how you look and how you sound. Specifically, audiences respond to your eye contact and eye movement. If you're not careful, and your eyes keep moving from person to person, that scanning will make you look "shifty eyed," and you'll seem to be dishonest or unsure.

During normal conversation, practically everyone gestures to describe movement, size, direction, etc., but speakers often "lock up" when talking to an audience. Use your hands to show them what you're talking about, don't just say it.

Be well balanced as you stand or sit and you'll look comfortable and confidant.

Shifting or rocking comes across as unsure and insecure.

Let the sound of your voice help you. Strong volume makes your voice not only louder, but also richer and fuller.

You'll sound more interesting and much more convincing. In order to maintain that volume, give yourself time to take a breath.

A pause also gives your audience a moment to process what you just said, and they'll stay connected with your ideas.

Talk only when you're looking at someone. Talk to people, not to things, and your words won't be wasted. Taking a breath and increasing volume will also help you get rid of those annoying non-words, too.

Use these techniques. They work. And imprint your own style and personality.

When Dr. King began his remarks that night in Connecticut he apologized for being a bit late. Severe weather had delayed his flight and made landing difficult.

When he said, "I was glad when we finally landed," a few people chuckled. He quickly added, "I don't want you to think I don't have confidence in the Lord in the air. It's just that I've had more experience with Him on the ground."

Meeting Dr. King that night was a powerful experience for me.

Use the skills he used, and you'll add to your experience and success as a speaker.

Staging Counts.

The senior managers of a medium-sized Midwest company scheduled a meeting of their top salespeople to recognize their accomplishments and to extend thanks for a job well done.

Their overall theme was, "We're all in this together, and everyone has played an important role in our success."

I was invited to help plan the meeting and to coach the executives who would be speaking. I welcomed the opportunity because I admired the company, its products, and its focus. Approximately 75 of the top producers from around the country were scheduled to attend the meeting at the corporate headquarters. I arrived the day before the event, and after meeting most of the scheduled speakers, I was taken to the auditorium where the meeting was to be held.

It was a very attractive room with seating for 100, a small raised stage, spotlights, projectors, PA system, lectern, etc. It had everything anyone could hope for in an auditorium. The room was already set up for the opening session next morning. Table, chairs, and a lectern were in place on the stage. The technicians dimmed the house lights and turned on the spotlight so I could get the full effect of the setting for the meeting. Everything was set for a first-class production.

After admiring the facility, though, I asked again about the purpose of the meeting. With great pride the CEO repeated it was "to bring everyone together and to show how we are all in this together."

I remembered that, of course, but I wanted him to say it once more. He meant what he said, and he was justifiably proud of his people and of all the teamwork which had produced such positive results. But then I asked him another question. With the house lights off, the auditorium was dark. The spotlights, however, illuminated the stage and the lectern.

My question was, "Does this look like 'we're all in this together'?"

He and his colleagues were silent for a few moments as they surveyed the situation. The staging of the meeting demonstrated a clear dichotomy. The executives would be brightly illuminated on stage, but everyone else would be sitting in the dark.

The staging said, "The important people, the leaders, will be up there in the light, but the followers will be down there in the dark."

The room produced a clear and definite separation! There was no "together." There was "us" and "them." That clearly wasn't the impression management wanted.

I asked if they would consider making a few changes to create the "together." They said yes, and we went to work. Here's what we did.

The tables, chairs, and lectern were taken off the stage and placed on the auditorium floor in front of the stage. The curtains were closed. The spotlights were turned off. The house lights were turned up full.

Now, everyone could see everyone. The speakers and the audience were on the same eye level. Everyone was on equal footing, and there could now be "conversation" rather than "proclamation."

The staging clearly demonstrated, "We are all in this together." That's what management wanted to convey, and that message resonated as soon as the participants entered the room. Before the first word was spoken, the staging itself conveyed a loud and clear message.

Of course, everyone still knew who the bosses were, but the staging produced dialogue and participation rather than silence and acceptance. Reports and evaluations from all participants confirmed that management had, indeed, communicated their message effectively. Everyone was truly in this together.

Everyone felt it, and everyone responded accordingly.

What was said during the sessions was important. *How* it was said was also important. But *where* it was said dramatically demonstrated the commitment to the message.

Everyone responds to how an event is staged. Because a meeting is a theatrical event, recognize and take advantage of the significance of staging. Have it support your words and reinforce your message with clarity and power.

What Can I Leave Out?

Most of us find it difficult to prepare and deliver a presentation no matter if it's business, social, or civic. That difficulty usually results from three specific problems: getting started, deciding what to include, and staying organized. The following ideas will help in all three areas.

Deciding on the first sentence will probably be difficult because we know so much about our topic. It's difficult to settle on that all-important major point. The solution is simple – don't try to identify that point too soon.

Rather, do this. Just write out rough notes about your general topic as quickly as you can. Don't be concerned with spelling, grammar, neatness, or punctuation. No one but you will see this piece of paper. Just capture as many ideas as quickly as possible without any thought of the sequence. This is like brainstorming, which works for one simple reason: tasks are separated. First comes collecting ideas, and then comes organizing.

When you're writing those rough notes, the first idea that comes to mind isn't necessarily the most important one. It's just the first one.

When the ideas stop flowing, think about your audience. Determine what they need to know and look back at the list you made. Which of the items will be most important to your audience? Those are the items to include in your presentation. Put aside all the others. You won't need them for this talk.

Maybe another talk at another time, with another audience, but not now.

Next, select the main point you want to make. Start your talk with that idea. Identify the topics related to the point you expect to cover, and list them in order. The resulting list is the outline of the scope and sequence of your presentation. At this point develop the notes into bullet points, but don't take the time to write complete sentences.

Now here's the key step. Look at the bullets and ask yourself this question. "What can I leave out and still make my point?" That simple question will make it much easier to construct your talk in a way that will attract and hold your audience. Plan to begin your presentation with a clear sentence identifying your main point – what you want your audience to do or to understand.

We refer to this as putting the message up front. Many speakers take too long getting to their message. When that happens, audiences become restless. They want "the point."

Once you've grabbed your audience, back up your position. Support it with evidence describing what happened in the past that led you to your point. Then deliver the final element of your talk. Tell them how you – or they – will succeed at doing or knowing what you are recommending. All of this material will focus on the future.

See how this sequence is so important and easy? First, describe the situation as it is *now*, then give background about what happened before now in the *past*. And finally describe what will happen after now in the *future*.

Keeping that timetable in mind will help you build and explain your position as well as assist the audience in tracking your thinking. They won't have to work hard to follow your reasoning.

And remember, if you ever make an audience work hard to follow your reasoning, they won't. You do the work.

So, there's the three-step process:

- Get started quickly by making rough notes;
- Select the items you'll need by defining the information your audience needs; and finally,
- Describe the present condition, the past events that caused the condition, and the future actions that will correct the condition.

Often, a simple strategy like this three-point plan can overcome daunting tasks like delivering a memorable presentation. This approach will make it much easier to prepare that next talk. Give it a try.

Use What You Have.

Whenever it's Academy Awards time there will be many categories honored, and the most important ones will recognize the performances of actors.

But what does this reference to actors have to do with business?

The comparison is easy. Businesspeople have exactly the same tools every actor has. Actors have their scripts and their bodies. Businesspeople have their scripts, their notes, and their bodies.

What's the difference, then, between how we respond to an actor's performance and how we respond to a businessperson delivering a presentation? It's focus and emphasis. I'm not suggesting businesspeople become actors, but I am suggesting they recognize why audiences respond to actors and then use that same focus and emphasis.

Many businesspeople focus only on data. However, sales are often made on the basis of impressions. Customers buy people, not just products.

Businesspeople should use their talents the way actors use theirs.

A colleague of mine once said to a group of business executives, "Use what you have." Then he went on to say, "If you're tall, use that; if you're short, use that; if you have a strong voice, use that. Don't try to be like someone else if you don't share the same characteristics. Do what works for you."

I added my own one-liner to his direction. "Whatever you do, do it on purpose." Let's see how that fits the actor/businessperson relationship.

Look first at the words. Every actor acknowledges that a good script is the basis of a good performance, and actors always seek out good scripts. The businessperson has a script or notes he or she wrote. Although someone else in the organization might prepare the actual text, the presenter is usually responsible for the content. In every case, it is the actor or the businessperson who delivers that content.

But here is a very significant point. Content alone is not sufficient. If the text were all that was necessary for a great performance, everyone could be an accomplished Shakespearean actor because everyone has access to the same words. Clearly, everyone is not an accomplished Shakespearean actor! What makes the difference? Interpretation. How the words are delivered makes for an excellent – or a poor – performance.

All presentations, whether on stage or in the boardroom have two components: the content and the delivery of that content. The actor uses all the tools at his disposal to make the script "come alive."

And he rehearses that delivery until he can seamlessly deliver the interpretation that produces the desired audience reaction.

What are those tools? His voice and his body. He controls how he sounds (loud, soft, fast, slow, articulate, mumbled, etc.) and he controls how he looks (eye contact, gestures, posture, movement, etc.). That's it! He has a script and body parts.

Now let's look at the businessperson. He or she has notes, the content, and the same body parts the actor possesses. The actor uses them with care and deliberation. The businessperson often ignores their importance. Businesspeople often "wing" a presentation. The actor, on the other hand, knows that the interpretation determines how an audience responds. And the actor rehearses to assure the accurate interpretation. The businessperson, likewise, should consciously interpret the words in order to determine how his customers and clients will respond, and he must rehearse.

In the current difficult business climate, the effectiveness of presentations can often provide distinct advantages when relating to the pressures of the marketplace. Now here's an important factor. Although it takes a long time to become a content expert, it can take only a matter of hours to learn the basic presentation skills and techniques. But then, of course, they require continuing practice, practice, practice.

A recent popular business book describes how a business can move from being "good to great." Acquiring the necessary physical skills can and will help anyone in business to move from being a good presenter to becoming a great presenter. By recognizing the importance of the delivery skills, seeking out the instruction, and carving out the time to practice those skills, businesspeople can and will increase their effectiveness.

When actors perform well, they are rewarded with trophies. When businesspeople perform well they are rewarded with contracts. That's a win for both parties.

It's Not Just the Words.

I begin with a story that makes an interesting point we can all take to heart. It goes like this:

The conductor of a symphony orchestra was auditioning pianists to fill a vacant position. Friends of a talented young man recommended him to the maestro, and the conductor scheduled an audition. When the young man arrived, he played the assigned piece – flawlessly. Every note was perfect, exactly as written. The friends were elated and certain he would be the new member of the orchestra. They were astonished, however, when the conductor didn't hire the young man.

When they asked the maestro to explain his decision, he responded this way: "You are correct. He played every note flawlessly. There wasn't a mistake in the entire composition. But we're not looking for someone who can just play the notes. We're looking for someone who can play the music."

Now, what does that have to do with business? Over the years I've had opportunities to attend a number of business and political functions where various professionals delivered speeches. Although a few of the presenters used notes and visuals, most of them read their prepared remarks.

They wanted to be sure to say precisely what they intended to say, leaving nothing to chance. Pretty typical in many business, academic, and political presentations.

And therein lies the problem. Most of them did a rather poor job.

Like the young pianist, they read each and every word – flawlessly, but there was no connection with their audience, no emotion, no passion, no "music."

No one will diminish the value and need to have the correct words in a speech, but in most instances, it is the delivery and the interpretation of the words that capture an audience. The emphasis, the pace, and the power of the delivery convert the words to ideas and conviction. Audiences respond to those qualities far more deeply than they do to mere words.

There's research to back up that statement. A study at UCLA demonstrated which elements of a presentation have the greatest impact on an audience. As important as words are, they account for only seven percent of the impact.

How the presenter looked and how the presenter sounded account for the other ninety-three percent. The words are important, but the delivery and the interpretation of the words get the audience to "buy in" or to "tune out."

For obvious reasons, I won't identify specific people or topics I observed, but I'll say, without hesitation, the presentations I sat through were just plain boring. The people were boring, not the material.

When planning to deliver a presentation, no one would deliberately ask himself, "What can I do to bore my audience to death?"

But, many people in various businesses, professions, and institutions accomplish precisely that. They convert good content into a poor experience for everyone. In every discipline, including business, communication is all about the exchange of ideas.

It isn't about trading words and simply pronouncing them correctly.

When you and your associates are called upon to deliver a speech or to read a prepared text, ask yourself, "How can I engage my audience?"

Then concentrate on the ideas rather than on just the words when you deliver your remarks. Audiences don't want someone who can just read accurately. If that's the case, give the audience a copy to read themselves. Cancel the meeting and send the speech via e-mail or snail mail. That will save a great deal of time because people can read faster than anyone can talk. And they can read at their own convenience.

Audiences don't want readers. They want someone who will make the words come to life. They want someone who will inspire them.

When you have the opportunity, or the need to read a prepared text, concentrate on delivering the ideas not the words.

Remember the comment of the conductor. "We're not looking for someone who can just play all the notes. We're looking for someone who can play the music."

The art of delivering ideas with conviction and passion is far more important than the skill of reading words flawlessly.

Here's a final thought. Parents read to their children at bedtime to put them to sleep. Reading still accomplishes that at a business meeting, a religious service, or an academic function.

What Should Your Visuals Look Like?

How many times have you sat through a business presentation where speakers used visuals, but you couldn't see them well because they were too small or understand what they meant because they contained too much data? Often there is more than one presenter, and that makes the situation even worse because all the presentations look the same.

When you are giving a presentation, here's a good rule to follow: If your audience can't see or understand your visuals, don't use them. That's pretty simple and straightforward, so what can you do?

Most speakers elect to use visuals because they attract attention and carry much information, but those two reasons can also cause problems for both the speaker and the audience. Because visuals attract attention, they compete with the speaker and, often, they carry too much information.

Whether you use low-tech slides and overhead transparencies or high-tech computers, here are a few suggestions for making and using visuals so they help both you and your audience:

First, don't put too much "stuff" on the screen. Your audience won't understand it. While you were preparing your presentation, you had plenty of time to think about and design your visuals, but your audience gets a quick look at the complete visual without time to study it. Make it easy for them to follow what you mean. You're the "show," and the visuals are your tools, so present information clearly and sparingly. If everything you intend to say is on your visuals, the audience doesn't need you. Cancel the meeting and mail them the visuals.

Assuming that's not an option, think about these guidelines for the three types of visuals used in business presentations: words, graphs, and pictures.

Words. Keep the word count down by using bullets rather than complete sentences. If at all possible, limit yourself to about 4 or 5 words per bullet and 4 or 5 bullets per visual. Use plain, bold letters and numbers that stand out clearly in contrast to the background.

Graphs. Keep these simple and uncomplicated. They usually show trends and comparisons related to numbers, and numbers can do only three things: They get bigger, they get smaller, or they stay the same. Instead of using hard numbers and spreadsheets during your presentation to show trends and comparisons, use graphs and charts. They are much easier for the audience to read and understand. Of course, have the hard numbers ready for the discussion that follows the presentation.

Pictures. These are worth the proverbial "thousand words." Even if you are artistically challenged, you can find good artwork on your computer to reproduce or use for appropriate graphics.

Other speakers on the agenda may use the same computer graphics package you use, so be careful your presentation doesn't look like all the others. If it does, you lose impact.

Second, many speakers use handouts, and they make the handouts and the presentation visuals look the same. Usually, this is a bad idea. What makes a good presentation visual doesn't necessarily make a good handout, and vice versa. Think of handouts and presentation visuals as cousins, not twins. There should be a family resemblance, but they aren't identical.

Here's something else to consider. Light colored text on a dark background is the easiest to read, however many speakers do just the opposite because they intend to print out the visuals, and everyone knows that requires a great deal of ink. That's not a good reason, but that's what speakers do.

Finally, during your presentation, whenever possible, avoid talking to the screen. Talk to your audience. They are the ones who deserve your attention and focus, and they are the ones who will respond to your presentation. The screen won't, so don't waste your words there. In many of our presentation coaching sessions, we emphasize, "Talk to people – not to things."

Follow these suggestions and guidelines, and your audiences will not only appreciate your work, but also understand your ideas.

And that's the reason for delivering the presentation in the first place, isn't it?

Start Your Engines.

Imagine you're sitting in an audience at an all-company meeting or at a professional conference. When the speaker is introduced, this is what you hear:

> "I'm pleased to tell you that the status of our company is strong and, with the strategies we have in place, it will become even stronger as we move through this next year."

> "Today I'll show you how to develop

presentation materials that will support your ideas as you want to display them – not as some unknown software developer thinks you should show them."

Both of these sentences would probably attract your attention from the very start of the talk because each one makes a strong and clear point. The content of each sentence "grabs" the audience because it relates directly to their interests. Both also preview the messages that will follow. Just as a newspaper headline gives an indication of the coming story, the opening of a talk should provide an indication of what is to come.

I borrowed a line from the automotive manufacturers for this item. They often describe good automobile performance in terms of going from a dead stop – zero – to sixty miles per hour in just seconds. Impressive!

A good presenter moves his audience from a standing stop to complete involvement in his talk in one sentence with no wasted time, resources, or energy. That's also impressive.

Both of the example sentences above do just that. They move the material and the experience from the full stop position just before the presentation started to "cruise speed" for the remainder of the talk.

The speakers, therefore, go "From Zero to Sixty in One Sentence!"

Many of us have said, or have heard others say, "I'm a little nervous when I start, but after a few minutes I'm fine."

At first glance that might seem appropriate, but there is an inherent problem with such thinking. If it takes that much time for a speaker to begin to do well, it means at the very start of his presentation he isn't doing his best work.

He is presenting a poor image at the beginning of his talk!

Since this is the first impression his audience receives, he must now overcome that negative before he has the audience with him. That makes his job even harder than he thought it would be before he began. Without a strategy it could take a long time for him to get to "sixty," and, worse case, he might not ever get there.

Every time you speak or write, other people judge you. And that judging begins with the first sentence you deliver. It's unfair to judge so quickly but, because that's what happens, be prepared for the judgment. Use a plan which will assure the judgment will be a positive one.

Presentations you give, no matter what the medium, the audience, or the location have three parts: What you say. How you say it. How you look when you say it.

It's like Neptune's Trident, his spear with three prongs.

It's interesting to note there are other sets of "threes" in presenting ideas that relate to both the content and the sequence of material.

The technique is called "The Rule of Threes" and reflects the fact that people tend to remember things in groups of three.

Consider: "Friends, Romans, Countrymen," "Life, Liberty, and the Pursuit of Happiness," "Of the people, By the people, For the people," "Larry, Moe, Curly," "Ho, Ho, Ho." I'm sure you can come up with many more, but these will do to make the point.

In every presentation, a speaker should focus on: The Beginning, The Middle, and The End. In other words, whenever you present any material, in any format, to any audience, pay close attention to: How you start. How you develop. How you conclude.

Although that might seem obvious, many presenters don't do any of those very well, and they certainly don't do them in that specific order because they don't have a plan. So, developing a plan and delivering a presentation that gets the results you want should be of primary concern.

With a plan, you'll get to cruise speed quickly, and you'll present a strong, positive image from your very first word. And you'll discover that you'll make your point quickly – and get the reaction you want.

In short, you'll get "From Zero to Sixty in One Sentence."

Ready. Set. Go.

When you're scheduled to give a talk, do you ever feel nervous at the thought of doing it? Your answer is probably, "Yes."

When you finally stand up to give that talk, do you feel the audience is judging you? Well, you're right! They are!

No matter the size of the audience, everyone is judging you, and they start the moment you're introduced – even before you begin to talk!

That doesn't seem fair, but that's what happens. So what can you do about it? Here are a few ideas to consider the next time you have to give a talk. They're simple, but they work. Before you start talking, do this: Remind yourself of the "mantra" we all used as children. "Get ready. Get set. Go."

First, decide what you're going to say. Do that by identifying the points you want to get across and to whom you will be talking. When you determine precisely what the audience needs to know, you'll be able to decide the specific content of your talk. Remember, the talk is for the audience, not for you. Pick what will be important to them, not just easy or convenient for you, and don't try to tell them everything you know. They don't want all that.

Once you've identified the content, you have another important element to master. Decide how to package and deliver the content because the judging we talked about is based on how you look and how you sound during the talk.

The content is part of the "Get Ready," of course, but now you're in front of your audience. What should you do? This might surprise you, but *don't* start talking right away!

Move to the place where you'll be delivering the talk, but don't say a word yet. When you reach that spot, take the next step: "Get Set." This means put your notes on the lectern. Be sure they are in the right order. If necessary, and possible, adjust the height of the lectern. Take a little half step back from the lectern so you don't hold on to it. Remember, the purpose of a lectern is to hold your notes, not to hold you! Stand up straight, evenly balanced on both feet, with your hands either at your sides or resting on the surface of the lectern. Don't lean on it. Just rest your hands there.

All of this is done in silence!

Now look at your audience and decide who you will talk to first. Pick a target! It can be anyone you want: the senior member, a friend, or a smiley face. But pick someone, and look him right in the eye.

You still haven't started talking!

When you have selected your target it's time to "Go." Deliver your opening sentence to that person in a strong voice. Take your time. When you get through that first sentence you'll feel you're on a "roll." Be conscious of your eye contact with your audience. If you're not looking someone in the eye, stop talking. Find another set of eyes and continue.

Talk only to people, not to things. Again, take your time. When you want to check your notes, stop talking and look at them.

When you use the time to take these steps and give yourself that license to be quiet, no one in an audience will think you're nervous. You may feel it, but they won't know it. An audience never "knows" how a speaker feels. The judgments we talked about at the beginning of this segment are based on the behaviors the audience observes.

When you look prepared, confident, and relaxed, you'll be able to control and direct the nervousness you feel. These skills and techniques will help you put that nervous energy to work to create a strong, professional impression.

Sure, the audience will still judge you, but their judgment will always be a positive one!

The Rule of Threes

Whenever you have the opportunity to deliver a talk in any venue – business, civic, or social – think in terms of "three."

Many business enterprises demonstrate the application of the Rule of Threes which illustrates how grouping items into clusters of three makes it easy to remember them. Even though most of us don't recognize it, we encounter, apply, and benefit from such groupings every day.

Think, for example of your telephone number, your

social security number, or your military serial number. Those long numbers are arranged in groups of three. Also, the Three Stooges, the Three Musketeers, and, of course, the Three Little Pigs.

On a more serious note, consider, "Life, Liberty, and the Pursuit of Happiness" or "Friends, Romans, Countrymen."

I used the word "opportunity" in the opening sentence because delivering a presentation should be thought of as an opportunity, not as a chore. A presentation is a chance to shine, to be in the spotlight.

Consider this: Most of what we do on our jobs isn't seen by our supervisors on any regular basis. They aren't looking over our shoulder checking on our progress. They might not even see us because we're working in a remote location, on the road, or at home. They assume we're doing our jobs, but they don't have first-hand evidence until we have a spot on the meeting agenda or on the platform.

That's when the evaluation happens.

What we do and how we do it during those few minutes has a powerful impact on a career path. Looking at the event that way, it's easy to see it as an opportunity. To make the best use of it, consider these three steps:

First, decide precisely what you want to say. That may seem obvious, but many people stumble at the start because they know so much about their topic – too much to include in a single talk.

Without focus, they talk too long and too fast.

Their audience gets lost, and sometimes annoyed. Not good for the career path.

Here's a way to make those critical choices by using "threes." Define your audience by asking: What do they already know? What do they need to know? How can my information help them?

Next, based on that audience analysis and all the material at your disposal determine the major points you want to make.

You won't have time to tell the audience everything you know, so don't even try. Select and edit.

Now you should be ready to construct your talk. It will have three distinct parts: the beginning, the middle, and the end.

Seems obvious, but many speakers start in the middle by providing detailed background evidence, anecdotes, and research data. Putting such information at the beginning is the wrong place.

Here's a better option. Draft your opening sentence, which serves two functions. It should "grab" your audience's attention, and it should preview what's coming. Then construct your closing sentence. Tell your audience what subsequent steps will be appropriate and expected.

Now that you have the "bookends" for your talk, it's time to fill in the supporting details. This is the place to provide the research, the anecdotes, and the background. By putting it here, in the middle, you have provided a context for your audience.

Using the "Rule of Threes" this way allows you to grab attention immediately, expand your concept with the necessary data, and finish with specific "marching orders."

Too often speakers seem to "run out of gas" at the end of a presentation because they aren't sure what they will say.

However, when you know what your last sentence is going to be, you'll be able to deliver it in a strong, confident-sounding voice.

That's the last thing your audience will hear from you so make it memorable.

That's always good for the career path.

Don't Just Say Something – Stand There.

People speak volumes even when they are silent. Sounds like a contradiction, but it isn't. All of us make instantaneous judgments about others the moment we encounter them. Think of a time you observed a stranger entering a room. You probably found yourself thinking, "I'd like to meet him or her" or "Let's see who else might be coming." Such decisions are based solely on visual information.

The lesson here is clear and simple. We judge others by how they look, and they judge us the same way, so it's important to convey the image we want by sending the "right" message. That image is often referred to as "Presence," a term increasingly popular in business. We've observed it in many other areas, including the military, where it's called "command presence" and in the theater where it's called "stage presence."

The question for all of us in business situations is, "How do I create that 'corporate presence,' that positive intangible impression?"

Here's the answer: We create the impression others have of us – an intangible – by controlling our behaviors – the tangibles. What we *do* sends clear messages. There are only a few behaviors to consider in creating those images, those impressions, those perceptions. Here they are: Eye Contact, Posture, and Gestures. That's it. Control those, and you'll project that powerful Corporate Presence.

Let's look at what we can do.

Eye Contact: In this part of the world, eye contact is essential if we want others to respond positively to us. If we don't look others in the eye, we are seen as evasive, nervous, weak, insecure, dishonest, and a host of other negatives. So the fix is easy. Look at people. Don't stare at them, *look* at them. Make your eye movements deliberate and controlled. "Take in" the entire situation and all the people. Connect with them.

Posture: Stand tall and straight with your weight evenly balanced. Move with a measured step. Take your time. If you walk too quickly, you'll seem nervous; too slowly, and you'll seem hesitant and insecure. Think of any sport you play or may have played in the past. You know full well that no one can play well off balance. The only time a player might be off balance is during time-out. Then no one cares. It doesn't count. As soon as it's play time again, balance.

Gestures: The third element of Presence is how you describe and emphasize your thoughts. In everyday conversation, everyone uses gestures freely without thinking about them. In conversation, no one plans gestures. They just happen, and they're always correct. When people are in the "spotlight," however, they tend to restrict movement. They grasp their hands in a "fig-leaf" position or in a prayerful mode. If you give yourself license to move, the correct gestures will come without even thinking about them. You'll look confident, and you'll feel better – more like yourself.

Let the gestures come from your shoulders – broad and fluid – just as you do in everyday conversation.

You will be seen as comfortable and confident.

Here's a final word about Presence.

Don't wait until you're scheduled to deliver a presentation to think about Presence. That could be too late because old habits die hard, and you want to project a new image. You are being observed and judged every time you're the focus of attention: when you approach a customer, when you welcome a new group of employees, when you make a sales call, or when you welcome a salesman into your office. During the first few seconds you appear before an audience in any venue, they will decide how they feel about you, so create the image you want.

Here's a guarantee. The behaviors you choose related to Eye Contact, Posture, and Gestures will definitely work for you – or against you.

Choose carefully and wisely. It's your choice – and your reputation.

Honor Time

"When I'm speaking at a program I like to be the first person on the agenda. That way, I can take all the time I want!"

A person in one of my "Effective Communication" programs said that on the second day when we were discussing honoring agendas. During the moment that I was formulating a response, another participant stood up, looked him in the eye, and said, "That's why everyone in this room thinks you're such a jerk."

Everyone did!

Paying attention to time is essential when delivering any kind of presentation because "Time" is a non-renewable commodity. You can't put poorly used time on a shelf in a plastic bag and take it down to use tomorrow. Once it's gone, it's gone. Certainly, every speaker's time is important, but anyone delivering a talk should be cognizant of the audience's time, too.

Here are some ideas to make presentations work well for you – and for your audience:

Start strong. Stand up straight, well balanced. Use a strong voice, and look the audience right in the eye.

Don't talk to the floor, ceiling, notes, or walls. Talk to people, not to things.

Know what your first sentence will be. Practice it before the event. Say it out loud at home, in your office, in the car, in the parking lot. Get used to how it sounds so you can speak it easily and comfortably. Shakespeare said, "Trippingly on the tongue." When your words flow smoothly, you make it easy for your audience to listen to you. Remember, your audience was paying attention to something else before you came on the scene. You have to get them to pay attention to you now. That first sentence might be a question, a statistic, a quote, or a direction. Just be sure it's relevant to your audience.

Know what your last sentence will be. Rehearse it, too. When you know how you'll finish, your volume will remain strong to the very end. The audience will see and hear you conclude, not just stop. That's the last thing they'll hear from you. Make it memorable.

Set ground rules. If you intend to take questions any time during the talk, tell them. If you want to cover all your material first, tell them that. It's your show. Make the time work for you. We've all seen presenters get side tracked, talking about something they hadn't intended to cover, and either run out of time before completing their material or talk as fast as they can just to get to the end. Neither choice works very well.

Make questions work for you. Sometimes questions can throw us off track by opening up issues not directly related to our topic. If that happens, do this: Be respectful and unemotional, rephrase or restate the question to keep it focused, answer it as well as you can, end the answer by saying, "That's why I'm suggesting we..." and restate your recommendation. That will get you back on track and ready to continue.

Use visuals – with caution. The audience is there to

see and hear you, not to read text and figure out your graphs and charts. Become a teacher at this point. You know what your visuals illustrate, but your audience doesn't know until you tell them. So teach them.

Get a Timekeeper. Have a colleague monitor time for you. You won't be an accurate judge of time while you're speaking, so get help.

Use your bookends. The first and last sentences are your bookends. No matter the length of the talk, those bookends remain constant.

If your timekeeper indicates you're running out of time, you can segue to your last sentence without any noticeable gaps in your sequence. Audiences appreciate and respect a speaker who can make his point and end on time.

Two traits we should all master.

Plan To Be Extemporaneous.

Planning to be extemporaneous isn't a contradiction. Business situations often require us to participate in discussions, to recommend actions, or justify positions. When we know in advance such an opportunity is coming, we take time to prepare by researching data and structuring our thoughts. We even rehearse what we plan to say.

But often we don't have time for all of that. We have to speak "off the cuff."

Here's the dilemma. Even without preparation time, we're expected to deliver a talk that is logical and sequential – one that's easy for our audience to follow.

Not only is that expected, but also it's in our own best interest to be able to do it. We've all admired people who can "talk off the cuff." Like many other things in life, some people are born with specific talents and others have to work at it. Even those with the talent, however, need a plan.

Whether you're a pro or a novice, here's a way to deliver a short extemporaneous presentation that is clear, concise, and complete – not to tell everything you know, but to make a point.

It's a simple four-step process.

Begin by taking control of the floor. If appropriate, stand up as you begin to talk so the audience can see you. You don't want to be a "voice in the wilderness." If that's not appropriate, sit up straight. The suggested script line is, "I have something to say about..." Announce your topic.

Tell the audience your point of view or position. The suggested script line here is, "I think we should..." In just a few words, state your position.

Present supporting evidence to defend your point of view. Without evidence, whatever you say will simply be an opinion. Of course, you're entitled to an opinion, but that's not very strong.

People shoot down opinions, and they have their own, but they can't deny conclusions based on documentation. Opinions alone aren't very convincing. (Unless you're the Chairman of the Board.) Suggested script lines here are: "The reason I say that is..." or "Because..." Then state your evidence.

Repeat your position. Since you voiced your position so quickly, some in the audience may not have caught it, so tell them again.

The suggested script line is. "That's why..." and say again what you said in step 2.

Now sit down or sit back in your seat. Your short speech is over.

Other suggested script lines include these:

For Step 1: "I'd like to say something about…" "Here's an idea…" "How about this…" Add your own.

For Step 2, options include: "I recommend…" "Let's…" "Here's an idea." Again add your own to the list.

Step 3 options are: "Because…" "Let me tell you why…" "For example…" Add your own.

Step 4 options could be: "So…" "Again, I recommend…" Add your own.

With all of these steps, make the language yours. Use words and phrases that are comfortable for you and that fit your usual language.

If the lines sound "canned," you'll come across as stilted – or phony and contrived – rather than sincere and convincing.

Here's the real value of this technique. You can present and defend a position in a matter of seconds. If others have a conflicting point of view, they must present ideas with supporting evidence as good as yours, or your position will prevail.

Also, if the others don't have a similar "script," they won't make their point as quickly and as clearly as you.

Business audiences admire and respect participants who can make a point quickly and clearly.

That ability demonstrates focus of thought and direction.

As you follow these few steps, keep this one additional point in mind.

Begin each step making eye contact with a different member of your audience.

Deliver each thought to a specific person.

Remember this rule. "To make your point, talk to people, not to things."

The Play's the Thing...

Whenever the Screen Actors Guild presents their Achievement Awards, I'm reminded of the following exchange. During a presentation techniques class, a participant "pushed back," and said to the instructor, "You're trying to make me into an actor. I'm not an actor. I'm a businessman."

Because of that attitude, further productive instruction was doubtful, so the instructor addressed the comment this way: "That's a valid concern, but let's put some ideas in perspective. First, there is a major difference between an actor and a businessperson. The goal of the actor is to become 'someone else.' The actor uses mannerisms, expressions, and movements to create the character in a production. The better he does that, the more convincing he is with the portrayal.

"The goal of the businessperson, on the other hand, is to present the 'best possible impression of himself' in order to develop genuine and positive working relationships with customers, colleagues, and clients. His behavior communicates his conviction and commitment.

"Are there any similarities between the actor and the businessperson? Yes. In order to practice his craft successfully an actor uses the two tools at his disposal: a script and a body. A writer has given him the words, and the actor uses his physical capabilities to deliver those words.

"What tools does a businessperson have at his disposal? He has two: a script (but he calls it notes or a speech), and he has a body. Precisely the same tools the actor has! The success of the actor depends upon how well he interprets the words in the script. He doesn't just 'say' or 'read' them. He communicates the ideas and the conviction.

And he rehearses the delivery with a director (his coach) until he is successful.

"The script alone is not enough for a successful performance.

With the businessperson, however, it seems the emphasis is just on saying or reading the words. He overlooks the significance of interpreting them. He works hard to get all the words "just right!" but he leaves little time for rehearsal and, unlike the actor, he often refuses the guidance of a coach.

All too often, the businessperson believes his audience will sit through his presentation no matter the quality of the delivery.

Bad idea!

"In a theatrical setting such behavior results in the audience walking out. In a business setting that behavior prompts an audience to tune out. Both reflect the evaluation of the overall performances."

So the presentation coach wasn't trying to make a businessperson an actor, but he was stressing the need for him to use the tools as well as the actor does.

The business presentation and the theatrical performance begin with the word and the interpretation.

After that, though, it's also important to consider the locations and the media in which the messages will be delivered.

An actor might work on stage, in television on radio, or in motion pictures. Each one requires a specific set of skills in order to be effective.

A brief example: Stage productions require bigger gestures than motion pictures do. In a live theater production, audiences are distant from the performer, but in a motion picture, close-ups are used. Likewise, voices must be projected more on stage than in a studio where there is amplification control.

(Increasingly though, stage productions are using wireless microphones to amplify actors' voices.)

Business presentations might be delivered in various settings including large or small audiences, webinars or conference calls. They may be planned or extemporaneous, live, or recorded.

That instructor was correct. It's important for businesspeople (as well as actors) to recognize the significant impact interpretation has on effective communication, to know the rules of their respective disciplines, and to master delivery skills in order to connect and influence their audiences.

One size doesn't fit all.

Bookend Your Material.

The next time you're scheduled to give a talk, consider these ideas in order to "bookend" your material. Plan the first and last sentences of the presentation to assure you're in control and to project confidence and conviction.

Speakers shouldn't expect audiences to work hard to "figure out" their content, scope, and sequence. Audiences are busy – and impatient. Most presenters, therefore, face three basic problems when planning a presentation: They know much more than any audience wants to hear. They're not sure how to select the necessary material. They're uncertain how to structure their presentation.

Presenters often think they have to include everything they know in order to convince the audience of their wealth of knowledge. That's risky. Audiences typically don't what to sit through a complete litany of information. That kind of "data dump" is usually annoying.

And often it's interpreted as an attempt to cover everything because the speaker isn't sure of anything. When there isn't a specific focus, audiences become restless. They want relevant information, and they want it *now*. If they don't get it *now*, they stop listening.

Heed these words from Dorothy Sarnoff. "Make sure you have finished speaking before your audience stops listening."

Incidentally, the same caution relates to writing. If your reader stops reading before coming to the end of what you wrote, you've wasted your time and lost an opportunity to influence their ideas. Don't "power pack" your material. Include only what you need. But, how do you determine that?

As a speaker, think like your audience. Ask yourself, "What interests them?" The answer to that simple question will direct you to select what is important to your listeners rather than comfortable for you. Once again, the same factors apply to effective writing. Become your reader. Why would someone take the time to read your words? What will your reader see as useful or valuable?

Now, what do you need to know to make the selection? Here are a few questions to get you started. What does the audience already know? Why do they need your information? How will they feel about your ideas? How much detail will they want? What's in it for them?

Answers to these questions, and others you add related to your specific business, will help you sort out and select the appropriate material.

Caution: Don't start writing your speech or paper right away. Write down ideas. What *might* be included? That information won't necessarily come to you in sequential order so when you're reviewing your notes, you might see that you don't need some of the items. That's good. Edit them out and sharpen your focus.

Now that you have that sharp focus, and you know what you want to tell your audience, set the order of the information. Decide how to begin, how to develop, and how to conclude. Start by making your point early in the presentation. Many speakers choose to lay out detailed background information in order to "set the stage" or to "soften up" bad news that might be coming later.

Both are interesting motives but, as we said earlier, audiences are impatient. They want to know the *What* of your presentation before they hear the *Why*. If you delay the *What*, audiences often become annoyed. So tell them what you want them to know, and tell them right away.

You're now almost ready to start your presentation, but there is one more detail. Decide what your first sentence will be, and what your last sentence will be. Write them down, and say them out loud. Don't memorize. Those two sentences are your presentation "bookends." The first one will "grab" audience attention quickly with a confident sound. Your voice will be strong, and your purpose clear. Planning the final sentence, likewise, will enable you to deliver the closing message in the same strong voice. You'll "conclude" with power, not just stop talking.

This "bookending" will frame and support your presentations. It will keep your audience engaged and paying attention until you finish speaking.

Shiny New "Things"

I was teaching a corporate communications seminar recently, when a participant asked a question after I had given an assignment calling for presenting a business related presentation to the class.

He asked, "Can I use my new tablet for the presentation?"

"Sure," I said. "But why do you want to use it?"

"It's really cool!" he said.

The response I didn't verbalize but thought about was to ask him, "Do you want to be cool, or do you want to be effective?"

Of course, it's possible to be both, but more often than not, there is a choice which reflects distinct differences. In most respects, the "technology de jour" is little more than an application of the garden hose analogy. If you put good water in one end, good water comes out the other end. If, however, you put dirty water in one end, dirty water comes out the other end.

The delivery vehicle is just that – a vehicle. Like a truck or an airplane, it carries something. The cargo is independent of the vehicle, and customers are more interested in the cargo than the carrier.

How does this relate to being "cool?" In developing any presentation, Step 1 is determining what you want to accomplish with your audience. There are two parts to that. First: What's your message? It's essential to identify what information you want to deliver. Write that down somewhere – a piece of paper or a computer screen – anywhere, but do it. If you can't write it down, you're not likely to communicate it clearly to your audience.

Now the part about the audience: What factors do you have to consider in order to assure that you'll get your message to each of them? And think of them as individuals, not as a group. As individuals, what do they know, expect, require, and value? What can you offer them? Again, write down your assessment and your conclusions. This will guide you to selecting the appropriate information and behaviors to deliver that carefully articulated and crafted message.

Now, it's time to ask the next question, "How can I do that?"

Selecting the medium should come at the end of the process, not at the beginning. Your selection will have an impact on how effective you'll be, not on how "cool" you'll be. There is little question that high tech delivery tools can be interesting and informative, but long before we had computers and tablets and LCD projectors, we used other delivery systems that were effective – and they still work!

There is an old saying in the visuals arts, "If the Special Effects are obvious, they'll distract from the story." In making your selection, ask yourself if you want a fixed sequence or if you will benefit from flexibility. If fixed is the better option, a computer presentation will certainly work well. But if flexibility is needed, consider using some of the old technology. Blackboards, flipcharts, and overhead transparencies are certainly low-tech, but you control every part of your presentation, and you can make adjustments based on audience reactions and changing dynamics.

Those tools aren't "cool," but they can be extremely effective. With up-front planning, you can apply the flexibility these tools provide because you always know where you want to go and what you have to do so your audience follows your lead.

There is yet another tool in the toolbox, but use it carefully. That's the Handout. It provides an excellent way to deliver details, but stay in control. As soon as you put something into someone's hands, that's where their attention goes. They'll turn pages ahead of where you want then to look, so give them only what you want them to have. Because you want the audience to pay attention to you, remain the center of attention and information.

These older tools may not be "shiny," but they'll

help you tell your story and be remembered as informative and professional, rather than "cool." In business, which one is more important?

Missing the Point or Missing the Target

Recently, I was listening to a couple of my friends argue over an exchange of e-mails. One said, "I don't think we should take the position you suggested. It doesn't make any sense to me"

The other responded, "You missed the point. What I said was we should…" He expanded, explained, and eventually clarified his position.

The argument heated up a little, but they finally resolved the misunderstanding and moved on to other topics. I thought about that response and wondered how often we hear the same thing in both our personal and business conversations. I also realized it's insulting to say that to someone!

Saying, "You missed the point," puts the blame for not understanding squarely on the shoulders of the listener or the reader. It says, "You're not smart enough to understand what I'm saying." The real blame, however, may rest with the speaker or the writer. If you hear yourself saying, "You missed the point," it could be that you missed the target. When someone doesn't get your "point," it may be because you didn't make it very well.

Here's something to think about. Many of us don't focus our messages well. When that happens, we blame others for not understanding us. We know what we mean and what we want, but we forget that the purpose of communication is to assure that someone else knows what we mean and what we want.

It's our responsibility to craft and deliver our messages clearly. I remember a quote from my first grade teacher that is appropriate here. "Say what you mean, and mean what you say." Good advice for a first grader, and good advice in business today. Every time I quote her, I recall an uncomfortable event that ultimately taught me a valuable lesson. Here's the story.

Many years ago I wrote a proposal for just a little less than a million dollars. It was the first big proposal I had ever written to a foundation, but I was sure we would get the funding because the company I was working for at the time could accomplish the task we described, and the idea behind the proposal was sound.

Another reason for my confidence was the fact that the program officer who would evaluate and decide on the merits of the proposal was a long-time friend of mine. We had gone to college together. This had to be good for our chances of receiving the funding, I thought. As I imagined events unfolding, here is what I foresaw. My friend, Ed, would come to my office and read my twenty-plus-page proposal. When he finished, he would close the proposal, put it down on my desk, reach into his pocket, and hand me a check.

Here's what really happened. Ed came to my office and read my proposal. He closed it and put it on my desk. So far so good, but my imagination was about to clash with reality.

Rather than reaching into his pocket and handing me a check, Ed leaned back in his chair and said, "That's interesting, Bob, but just what is it you want to do?"

With a combination of annoyance and surprise I started to come out of my chair and said, "I want to…" and I explained the idea in one sentence.

He responded with, "Why didn't you say that in the proposal?"

I sat down. I had just learned a hard lesson. The idea of the proposal was clear in my mind, but it wasn't conveyed well on paper. When I was challenged, I articulated it in one clear, focused sentence. But that sentence wasn't in my proposal.

After Ed left, I rewrote the proposal, and I was sure to include that sentence more than once in the new version.

Eventually, we did receive the funding because the idea was sound and the company could carry out the task.

But the award had nothing to do with having gone to college with Ed.

Although our relationship did give me the opportunity to resubmit the proposal rather than having it simply rejected, we often don't get second chances in life.

Ed hadn't missed the point when he read my proposal. I missed the target when I wrote it. He did me a favor. He taught me a valuable lesson which I'll always remember. I hope you'll remember it too.

If you don't hit the target, you can't expect anyone to get your point.

CHAPTER 2

Managing

Teach others what to do. Teaching requires explanation, demonstration, correction, coaching, and reinforcement. It is extremely active, and it must be clearly visible to all parties. An effective teacher is a role model who opens paths and expectations. That requires visibility. A manager leads by example – not by words alone. Shows others what to do.

Getting others to do what you want them to do is perhaps the most difficult task in the workplace. Most workers learned to perform a task that was integral to the work they were doing. They learned to be good "doers," and when they became good at that, they were eventually promoted to become managers.

The problems started when they didn't know how to guide the behaviors and performance of others. As soon as something went wrong with how staff members were doing their jobs, the new managers jumped in and fixed it. They became "doers" again rather than managers.

Managers are teachers, and they must learn entirely new ways to behave. This section describes a wide range of examples and options that are effective in the workplace. They'll illustrate how to get work done through the talents and participation of others. It includes reviews of such requirements as defining the tasks to be completed, determining and providing resources, establishing timelines, allowing for reasonable errors, and providing feedback on progress. Knowing about those options and seeing the impact they have on workers will make the position of "manager" more productive and rewarding for all the parties involved.

Delegate It or Do It?

We all play many roles as we work through our business lives. Sometimes we are responsible for carrying out tasks, but at other times our primary role is to get other people to do things. These different roles require different behaviors.

Let's look at them.

First, the role of "doer" on the job. When we began our careers, our main function was to do something: build displays, teach classes, drive trucks, audit books, etc. We had to master specific skills. With diligence and practice, we got better and better at doing our jobs.

As we gained experience we took on more responsibilities and expanded our skills. We knew precisely what was expected of us. Often, the knowledge we brought to the job was improved and expanded by additional training and instruction. We learned to be better and better "doers." That was good.

For many of us, though, when we got really good at

doing something, we were promoted to a new level of responsibility. We became managers and, suddenly, everything changed. No longer were we expected to do the things we were good at. The new job required us to get other people to do those things. The skills and information we needed on the new job were entirely different from our former role.

What worked for the doer usually didn't work for the manager. Compounding the problem was the fact that nobody taught us how to manage! We had learned how to do things, but we didn't know how to get others to do those things.

As managers, we need to master a new set of skills, and one of the most important ones is knowing how to delegate. Here are a few points to master. To be an effective manager: Help your staff understand what must be accomplished. Encourage them to participate in appropriate decision making. Allow them to make acceptable mistakes.

Here is an example of good delegation. It includes all of these elements.

I have a friend, Larry, whose daughter got her driver's license a couple of weeks before the family was going to visit relatives in an adjoining state. His daughter asked if she could drive. Larry said, "Yes."

With that one word he had delegated the driving responsibility to his daughter. She studied maps and planned the route. On departure day, she got behind the wheel, eager to begin the journey. Her mother was at her side. Larry got into the back seat with a newspaper, and said, "Okay. It's all yours."

Off they went. From the back seat, Larry was watching closely, but he didn't offer any advice. This was her opportunity to grow, and she was doing fine. Eventually he realized at the speed she was going and the lane she was in, she was probably going to miss an exit they had to take. He now had a dilemma. Did he become a "doer" and tell her about the potential error? Or did he let her make the mistake? According to Larry, the hardest part of the trip was watching in silence as she drove past the exit.

In a short while his daughter discovered the error, stopped the car, checked the map, turned around, and got them to their destination. It was an hour later than planned, but they got there safely. She had been a good "doer," and she became a better and more mature driver. She had a positive experience, and she achieved an important goal. At the same time, Larry had been a good delegator by allowing her to make an acceptable mistake.

He told me if she had been heading off a cliff he would have intervened quickly, of course, but just missing an exit was an "acceptable" error. That's what delegation is all about.

Let's do a little self-evaluation. At home and on the job are we a "doer" or a delegator? Which should we be? What difference will it make?

Walk the Walk – What the Heck is That??

Some sentences don't make any sense. "Walk the Walk" is one of them. But when something is repeated often enough it becomes accepted as correct, even if it's wrong. This is like the "big lie" technique. Just say something again and again, and it becomes "true."

"Walk the Talk" was the original version of the "walk the walk" sentence, and it made sense. "Walk the Talk" distinguishes between doing something and just talking about doing something.

"Walk the Talk" was an undisputed compliment because it recognized that when a person did what he said he would do, he was respected and admired.

More and more, in business, in industry, and certainly in government today we're experiencing talk that isn't backed up by action. Too many people just "talk the talk."

As children we were told, "Talk is cheap." As adults, we know that's still true. The lasting mark of any person is what that person does.

It's not just the words he speaks. Many "leaders" in business and politics talk a good line, but they don't follow through. Their words display eloquence, but their actions demonstrate a lack of commitment.

Where there is a contradiction between words and actions, most thinking people pay attention to the action. It's easy to find those contradictions between the TALK and the WALK. For example:

- A former US VP talks about saving the environment and conserving energy but, "He lives in a 10,000-square-foot, energy-guzzling mansion." (From the book, *Walk the Walk* by Alan Deutschman)
- The US public is urged to buy small, energy-efficient cars, yet government leaders use fleets of SUV's for official functions.
- The public is told to conserve and to spend money wisely, but congressional leaders continue to delegate "earmarks" for their constituents.
- Government leaders swear an oath to "Preserve, Protect, and Defend the Constitution," but many then describe it as a "living document" and work to change it.

I'm sure you can add many more to this list.

Businesses and individuals are expected – required – to pay taxes or face severe penalties, yet many of our "leaders" don't pay theirs – and they are absolved of any wrongdoing.

Certainly, words can inspire action, and that's good. But it's the action that makes the difference, not the words. As a means to an end, words are excellent, but, as ends in themselves, they are hollow and meaningless.

Eliza Doolittle had it right in *My Fair Lady* when she sang, "Words, words, words, I'm so sick of words—Show me."

When *Talk* is followed by action – by *Walk* – we have a powerful direction. If someone were simply to "Talk the Talk," nothing would be accomplished. Indeed, such a person would reflect Shakespeare's ideas where he had Macbeth describe, "…a poor player that struts and frets his hour upon the stage and then is heard no more. It is a tale told by an idiot, full of sound and fury, signifying nothing."

All too many in business, and in politics, "strut and fret," but it's the doers who truly lead. In every one of the eleven sections of his book *Walk the Walk*, Alan Deutschman himself describes how "…leaders need to inspire belief through their actions." That describes, "Walk the Talk."

Why he selected the title he did is anyone's guess. It signifies nothing. Many years ago a colleague gave me a framed picture of a turtle. Under the picture was this in-scription. "Behold the turtle. He makes progress only when he sticks his neck out." That's commitment. That's action. So, in your business and personal lives continue to talk, debate, and to discuss, but don't stop there. Follow the talk with action.

My first grade teacher summed up this concept in

these nine words, "Say what you mean, and mean what you say." That was good advice then, and it still applies today. So, don't just talk the talk, don't just walk the walk (whatever that means), but follow this clear direction: Walk the Talk. That speaks volumes to all of us, and that motto belongs on the desk of every business and political leader.

Earlier I mentioned a couple of things from my childhood, but I can't remember anyone ever playing a game called, "Follow the Talker." Can you?

The Infinite Workday

An old adage tells us about not being able to see the forest for the trees. Here's an updated version. We don't see work-life changes because we're part of them. An example: Not too long ago there was general agreement about what the term "workday" meant. Although the specifics varied from business to business, it was understood that the workday began sometime between 6 and 9 in the morning and ended sometime between 4 and 6 in the evening.

Today, that's completely different. The workday can now encompass what current jargon refers to as 24/7. Technology made the change possible, and our acceptance of that technology encouraged the change. Now the change is part of our lives.

I realized that recently when I was checking and responding to e-mail late Saturday night and it dawned on me it was late Saturday night! I was working and responding to other people who also were working late Saturday night. In past years it certainly wasn't unusual for people to take work home, but the limits of the traditional workday have now disappeared. Information moves all day and all night, and we expect others to respond to our messages. Also, we're expected to respond to theirs, no matter when they arrive. That's just the way business is these days.

I'm not taking a position pro or con on this issue. I'm just looking at it differently now. We no longer have to be in a specific place during designated times to be "at work." This is a good news/bad news situation.

Recently, an acquaintance shared this story with me. He went on a long planned family vacation with his wife and two young children. As many of us have done, he brought along his laptop and his cell phone. Usually we do this to keep in touch with the office, but he did it to keep his job at the office. His company was downsizing, and he didn't want anyone to know he was away. He felt his absence might lead to him becoming a victim of the cuts. Technology kept him in the loop all the while he was "on vacation." I put those words in quotes because the other side of the story is the fact that, to his wife and children he was always "at work." That's the good news/bad news aspect I mentioned. Physically he was with the family, but mentally he was at the office.

This all becomes a matter of setting priorities, allocating resources, and viewing circumstances from different perspectives. Corporate executives have often leveled criticism that employees spend company time doing personal tasks on office computers. No doubt, there is some of this, but what is often overlooked is the amount of time employees spend on their home computers doing company work. A recent study of 500 subjects from around the country, however, reported that workers spend more of their personal time at home doing office work than they spend at the office doing personal tasks.

I'm not advocating or excusing taking advantage of

company facilities, but I think the results of the survey and the recognition of our own behaviors might provide a different way of looking at today's work force and the new "infinite workday."

There is no question that a national sample of only 500 workers is small, but as we all consider both the survey results and the time we spend on our own computers, we'll probably agree that the traditional concept of the workday has changed. We aren't restricted by time or place any more, and we have accepted and adapted to the changes.

That change certainly deserves considering this question. What effect is this change having on each of us, on our employees, and on our personal relationships?

A Good Manager Should Be a Good Teacher.

When anyone moves into the new role of being a manager, behavior and attitude must change in order to successfully carry out the new duties and responsibilities. One of the most significant changes requires a shift in focus from being a "doer" to being a teacher. "Doers" perform tasks, but managers – teachers – assist and guide others to perform those tasks. Good teachers don't focus on teaching. They focus on students learning, and that difference of perspective is significant. For example, if someone focuses on the task of teaching, what is done, how it is done, and when it is done are all at the convenience of the teacher. On the other hand, if the focus is on learning, then what is done, how it is done, and when it is done are all for the benefit of the student. That simple change of perspective results in vast changes of behavior.

In a classroom, when a student masters a concept, a

fact, or a principle, the teacher has been successful. Student success is the reward the good teacher seeks. In business, a manager should provide the tools, the opportunities, and the skills to assist his staff to grow and develop.

No manager can, nor should he attempt to, perform all the tasks necessary to run a business. Although he might know how to do them, he should let others perform the jobs. The good manager is confident that his staff knows what to do and how to do it and, collectively, they all contribute their individual talents to the overall success of the business. A good manager, like a good teacher, encourages and enables other individuals to contribute their talents in a way that will be successful for everyone and, by extension, for the business.

Here are a couple of ways to look at being an effective manager. In the first analogy the manager is like the captain of a ship. The captain has the big picture, knows the destination, the route, and the procedures to follow. The captain can't work in the engine room, the radio room, and the dining room all at the same time. Others have to do those jobs.

Of course, the captain knows what those jobs require and what support is necessary, but he keeps his hands off. He assumes that others will carry out their responsibilities, and he delegates those tasks. But he doesn't do the work. If he devoted any of his time to doing the actual work, he would place the entire ship in jeopardy because no one would be attending to the "big picture" of operating the ship safely. Without the full participation of the entire crew, however, the ship might not reach its destination regardless of the knowledge of the captain.

Here's another brief analogy. A manager is like the conductor of an orchestra. The conductor knows the musical score and what effect he desires. Further, the conductor knows what each instrument and what each musician is capable of doing. The conductor calls upon each member of the orchestra to contribute the unique sound his instrument can produce. The combination and interaction of all the instruments contribute to the ultimate success of the performance. The conductor doesn't play all the instruments, but he knows what they can do, and he uses the experience, understanding, and talent of the entire orchestra to achieve the desired result.

The successful manager, likewise, must guide, teach, and lead. The primary focus of the successful manager should be to accomplish all the designated tasks required of the business while developing the staff and assuring that they all contribute their individual talents.

The captain uses knowledge and experience to enable the crew to do their jobs so all of them can reach the designated port safely. The conductor uses talent, creativity, and encouragement for the listening pleasure of the audience. The successful manager uses his knowledge to meet the challenges and opportunities of his business responsibilities.

Knowledge, sensitivity, ability, creativity, and experience all contribute to being a ship's captain, an orchestral conductor, a successful manager, or a professional teacher.

Quite a list of responsibilities, but quite an array of rewards!

The Performance Review Is a Process, Not an Event.

We've all lived through a performance review. Either someone did it to us, or we did it to someone else.

They are necessary, but often reviews are uncomfortable, unpleasant, or unproductive. When done well, however, they can be helpful to both parties.

If you're in a position to review the performance of others, here are a few suggestions that should make the job easier and the outcome better. When you're the one being reviewed, these suggestions will also be helpful because you'll have a better idea of the steps in the process.

First, think about the title of this segment. *A Performance Review is a Process, Not an Event.* Sure, a time will come when you sit with the person you're reviewing, but if you do your job well, that meeting will be just one step in an ongoing process. When the meeting happens, there should be no surprises to either party.

Let's look at the whole thing. You can conduct a good review session only if you have specific material to discuss. That means you have to gather performance data on a continuing basis. Data should include both positive and negative information relevant to the position. Observe, question, listen, document, check, and organize that information. This is just another application of the communication skills we've discussed in the past.

We need to be clear and specific when we discuss performance. If you concentrate on what your employee "does," your meeting will stay on track and will move in a clear direction. If you aren't specific, you might get side tracked. For example: If you say to an employee, "You've been coming in late too often" or "You'll have to complete your assignments sooner," you're likely to get a defensive response. You'll hear, "No later than anyone else" or "I get my work done."

Now you have a problem because your words were vague. That makes it difficult to stay on track, and the discussion could turn into an argument because you have one perception, but your employee has another. On the other hand, look at the difference if you are specific. "You punched in fifteen minutes late last Monday, Tuesday, and Thursday" or "You'll have to get your assignments in by 3:30 every Friday afternoon." There is no wiggle room with these sentences, and you both can discuss facts not interpretations. Focusing on specifics will keep the conversations on track. That's why continual observation is essential. You have to know the facts in order to talk about them.

Here is another specific communication technique. As you near the end of the session after you both have agreed on future performance, ask your employee questions like, "What can you do to accomplish this?" or "How do you think this should be done?" or "What do you think you should do first?"

The emphasis here is on the word "you." When an employee has to respond to this type of question, the ideas and the directions are his, not yours. When an employee describes his own future behavior, he's more likely to do it. If you say, "I think you should…" your employee might agree in order to end the session, but he will likely have limited buy-in to your suggestion. Get the employee to suggest the solution, and he'll be more likely to commit to it. Of course, as the manager, you have the ultimate responsibility to be sure the suggestion is appropriate. With this technique, you are directing the discussion, not turning over your authority.

After the session, continue to observe, question, listen, etc. because this is what continues the process.

During those subsequent observations, give praise where appropriate and add this: ask, "How did you do that?" or "How did you come up with such a novel solution?"

Then listen to the answer.

When you do this, you compliment the employee and encourage additional dialogue that demonstrates that you really do listen and that you respect the contribution of the employee. The dialogue and the process continue. That's why there will be no surprises at the next session. Both of you participate in the dialogue that will continue long after the review session and long before the next meeting.

Here comes a shameless personal plug. There's a lot more about Performance Reviews in my book, *Becoming a Successful Manager* (McGraw-Hill). You might want to take a look at it for additional ideas.

Hiring the Right Person Means Getting the Right Information.

Hiring the right person for a position can be a difficult task and, all too often, interviewers make the wrong choice. Selecting the best candidate is an exercise in good communication, so let's look at the process and how we can be more focused and productive.

The responsibility of the Interviewer is very clear: it's to select the best candidate from the available pool. Here are some specific skills to use and steps to take in making the best choice.

Begin by deciding precisely what you are looking for. You have to be specific here or the rest of the process will be trial and error, and we all know how costly that can be. Write down what skills and abilities the candidate must have in order to do the job successfully.

There are two important elements in that last sentence. First, you have to concentrate on actions and not get caught up in feelings and personalities. When you hire someone, your main objective is to select a person who can do something. There is a role to play, and there are tasks to accomplish. Write down what that "something" is.

The second element is the act of writing. Write down the specifics, don't just think about them. A blank piece of paper is a harsh taskmaster. That's why I'm making this suggestion. If you can't write down what you want, you probably aren't sure of what that is, and you probably won't get it. Use the discipline of the blank piece of paper at the start of the hiring process, and you're much more likely to select the right person. The reason is simple.

If you can write down precisely what you're looking for, you'll see it when it appears.

When you know exactly what you're looking for, you're ready to review applications and resumes, conduct interviews, and make your selection. Remember that old adage, "Be ready, willing, and able," because it's going to work here. Let's take those three items in reverse order.

Be Able. You can determine what a candidate is able to do by looking carefully at the resume. That's all past history. It deals with performance, and that's what you're looking for.

Since you have determined exactly what you want the candidate to do, the resume will help you determine if the applicant has the skills you need. If the resume doesn't show those skills, no further contact with that candidate is necessary.

This will save time for you and for the prospective candidate. Speaking of time, review the resume before the interview. Don't waste time reading during a scheduled interview. Use that time for conversation.

Be Willing. During the interview, listen for clues

about the candidate's interest in contributing to your company or department. Listen for comments like, "I'd like to..." or "I look forward to the possibility of..." or "If I could..." The interview suggests future possibilities, whereas the resume described the past.

Be Ready. Here is where maturity and personality enter the picture.

You must determine if the candidate will blend into the existing organization.

Will the candidate become a good member of the team and be able to use his skills in a productive way? The candidate isn't going to be a corporate hermit, so interpersonal qualities are important.

You can see the communication focus throughout this process.

Begin by writing clear and specific descriptions of what you want.

Then ask questions related to the candidate's ability to deliver those specific skills. Finally, listen carefully to not only what the candidate says during the interview but also to how he says it.

There is a lot more about this process in the book I co-authored with Gary Grossman.

You might want to take a look at *Becoming a Successful Manager* for some additional suggestions.

The entire hiring process is important, of course, and all the steps are necessary in order to hire well. However, that first step we discussed, being clear about what you want, is essential.

It's the old story about taking a road trip in your car. If you don't know exactly where you want to go, any old road will do.

You'll use up a lot of time and gas, but you won't accomplish anything. What's the point to that?

Business and Battles

On Armed Forces Day, I found myself thinking about what we all have and why. It took a lot of hard work and sacrifice to develop this country as well as effort to produce our business world. It isn't a perfect business world, but it's been good to us and for us. We owe much to the many who have gone before us, and we can benefit from their experiences.

I found some quotes related to the military, and I realized with only minor adjustments those quotes fit right into our business world. I invite you to consider them and to make your own connections.

General George C. Marshall said, "Don't fight the problem, decide it." It's interesting that some business people avoid making difficult and unpopular choices. With fingers crossed, they hope the problem will just go away. Usually it doesn't.

General Tommy Frank said this about hope: "Never let 'hope' be a strategy." Sound managing philosophy in six words.

Ignored problems get bigger and more complex until someone finally makes a decision. The advice for all of us is simple.

Little problems are easier to solve than big ones. It's much easier to extinguish a campfire than a forest fire. That's not a military quote, but no one can argue with the validity of the message.

Delegating tasks and responsibilities is difficult for many business people.

Here's a quote from someone most people think of as a hard-nosed, dictatorial leader, General George S. Patton.

This is something he believed in strongly, and which certainly contributed to his military success, "Never tell people how to do things. Tell them what to do, and they will surprise you with their ingenuity."

That's hard for many managers to learn (some never learn it), but following the General's advice can open up a world of options individual managers might never identify themselves. We all work with people who are smart and creative. Let those qualities work for you as a manger.

Patton also said," No good decision was ever made in a swivel chair." Of course, that's an exaggeration, but it does present an interesting idea for later discussion.

Staying with decision-making for a moment, here's something else to consider: General Norman Schwarzkopf said, "The truth of the matter is that you always know the right thing to do. The hard part is doing it." My guess is that most of us have wrestled with that kind of situation in our business and personal lives.

In business, and in the military, being a team leader is difficult.

Here's a perspective from General Dwight D. Eisenhower. "Leadership is the art of getting someone else to do something you want done, because he wants to do it." Think about that the next time you encounter managerial problems.

Goal setting is another important element of leadership, and General Eisenhower set a very clear goal for the troops just prior to the Invasion on June 6, 1944.

He said, "We will accept nothing less than full victory!"

Any questions?

As in warfare, all of us must constantly prepare for and cope with competition. If we don't prepare and we aren't vigilant, we risk losing market share and possibly an entire business.

In military terms, as well as civilian situations,

George Washington said, "One of the best ways to keep the peace is to be prepared for war." Although we don't engage in actual combat with our competition, we do compete. So we must always be prepared, strong, and ready.

Speaking of competency and being ready to take advantage of developments, here's a final quote.

I like this one because it sets the stage for competition and reality.

This comes from a U.S. Infantry Manual. "If the enemy is in range – so are you." Our competitors are as close to us as we are to them.

To all members of the Armed Forces – Past, Present, Future – Thanks for your service.

Compromise Is Just One Option.

Media coverage is often filled with the word "compromise" in relation to the federal budget. The financial condition, of course, is serious and is being played out on a national stage because of the conflicting positions held by the various political parties.

Business and personal relationships, however, face similar problem-solving requirements every day. Although not national in scope, those conditions are significant to everyone involved. Compromise, however, isn't the only method for resolving business and personal conflicts. It might not always be the best one either.

This old adage might provide some direction here: "If the only tool you have is a hammer, everything looks like a nail."

Resist the temptation to approach every problem from the same perspective. In order to match the tool to the task, here are five options to consider when faced with conflict situations.

Avoid. Sometimes a topic isn't worth the time or attention to engage. The motto, "Pick the hill you want to die on" comes to mind here. Some differences simply don't deserve attention, and you may elect to avoid the conflict and move on to other issues. That behavior, however, may be interpreted as agreement with the other position. If you don't want to send that message, state your opposing position clearly, or elect this next option.

Compete. Take a firm stance and use all the tools at your disposal to "win" the conflict. The aim here is to have your position prevail. In matters of principle, morals, and ethics, you may elect to draw the proverbial line in the sand and hold firm, no matter what consequences. Life is filled with winners and losers, and only one side can win. That's what competition is all about, but if you don't want to compete, you can always elect the next option.

Accommodate. Give in to the other competitor. Some companies just cut their losses and get out of a business. That's often seen as a weak position, but it isn't necessarily so. If you make that choice, so be it. It's yours, and there's nothing wrong with accommodating from a position of strength. As the gambler in the song said, "Know when to hold 'em, and know when to fold 'em."

So far, in all of the options, there has been a winner and a looser, but if you want to "make a deal" select option number four.

Compromise. In this situation all parties give up or lose something. At the conclusion of a compromise, no parties have all of what they had at the start of the discussion. You keep what you "must have" and agree to give up what you can "do without." No party truly "wins" in a compromise, so you must decide what you are willing to give up. In a compromise, the battle lines are drawn, and each party works to push back the other side. No one ends up at the initial position.

This final option may be optimal in many business situations and certainly with personal relationships.

Collaborate. With this option: the discussion begins with a blank page and a shared question, "What can we do together to resolve the situation?" Step one is usually a clear definition of the situation so both sides understand and agree on the specific problem and the desired goal. With that done, the task becomes one of deciding precisely "how to do it." Everything is equally likely. All decisions are written down to avoid later misunderstandings. The parties don't move forward until the language is clear and agreed to by all participants.

No question, this can be time consuming and stressful, but it produces results both parties can accept and defend.

Interacting with customers, colleagues, and family members is always complex. Considering these five options and deliberately picking the most appropriate one before acting can be a sound tactic. Remember that old adage. "Look before you leap." Seems to fit here, doesn't it?

Choices

Every day, we make choices. Changing business climates and economic pressures demand we evaluate our practices and communicate our priorities. All too often, those choices are clouded in ways that result in our becoming distracted.

My book, *Mottoes for Managing*, includes two examples which illustrate such misdirection. This first one examines the differences between *Movement* and *Progress*.

A former associate of mine once operated a successful business. I use past tense because the business is no longer as successful. He has lost a significant share of his market. Here's why. When he started, he looked for new opportunities. He opened new markets with new ideas and new services. But his ideas and services didn't remain "new." He kept doing what he knew how to do, and he did it in ways he knew always worked for him. Competitors saw his success, repeated it, and then improved upon what he had started, but he continued to do what had traditionally worked for him. He epitomized that old comment, "I know what I like, and I like what I know."

For a while, he held his position in the market, but slowly his competitors caught up to him and, eventually, moved ahead of him.

He still had a good product, but it was suited for yesterday's market! He remained firm in his convictions and in his business practices. But since the competition was moving forward, by comparison, he was moving backward. Today, his business is but a fraction of what it once was.

The second example illustrates evidence of another business problem: *Activity* rather than *Achievement*. People at all levels of organizations are busy doing many things but accomplishing very little. Sometimes the questionable activity is the result of a lack of employee focus and, sometimes, faulty business procedures result in the nonproductive activity.

Let's examine the lack of employee focus first. Look at the way offices and cubicles are arranged. Usually, from the outside it's difficult to see the screens of the omnipresent computers.

Managers have no idea what is being accessed, but employees look very busy. There's plenty of activity, but the increasing use of personal e-mail and Internet surfing during business hours diminishes productivity. Move the computers – see what happens.

Now look at a questionable corporate practice. Many sales related organizations require sales people to make a specific number of telephone calls to clients every day. They are measured and evaluated on the basis of the number of calls, but that might be the wrong factor to measure. The number of sales completed should be the important criterion, not the number of calls made. Successful salespeople know that extended conversations and contacts are often necessary in order to build relationships that lead to sales.

When managers assume that the number of calls is the primary determiner of success, they are playing the percentage game. If sales people have to be monitored to be sure they make a specific number of calls every day, maybe the managers hired the wrong people in the first place.

Such a corporate focus might also mean the wrong managers were hired because they are concentrating on activity rather than on achievement.

These two examples illustrate just some of the choices we have to make every day in our businesses. Choosing between *movement* and *progress* or *activity* and *achievement* is necessary, but often the distinctions aren't clear. The options are often confused because, at first glance, they don't seem to be very different, but they are worlds apart. In order to minimize that confusion, try changing your perspective a bit by asking yourself these two questions. The choices will then become easier to make. Do I want to get somewhere, or do I just want to keep on moving? Do I want to accomplish something, or do I just want to be busy?

We live with the consequences of our choices, so be sure to make the right ones, not just the expedient ones.

Leveling the Playing Field

The phrase, "Leveling the Playing Field" is interesting. It's intended to indicate an activity which makes everything equal. Seems like a good idea but, in reality, in order to achieve the appearance of equality, the entire field must be lowered. When the dirt is distributed to level the field – to smooth out the highs and lows – the end result is a lower field. The peaks fill in the valleys, thus lowering the level.

When used to describe competition then, the phrase could be changed to "lowering expectations." When used to describe intellectual challenges, it could be restated as "dumbing down." The heights are no longer high. The once outstanding elements become just like everything else.

We have to ask, "Is that an improvement? When everything seems the same, but a bit lower, what have we accomplished?" When the high points are lowered to that secondary level, "Leveling the Playing Field," is nothing more than an illusion of improvement.

There is another illusion worth recognizing in various settings in business and government. It's called "Perceived Power."

It occurs when people *think* someone has power or authority even when he or she doesn't. An affiliation or a personal contact can be sufficient to convince others that someone is "important."

"Just plain folks" can acquire authority, even though they haven't earned it or deserve it, simply through perception.

Here's an example that illustrates the concept of perceived power. At one time I was a member of the Governor's staff in Illinois. Because of my assignment, my business card indicated, "Office of the Governor." Sounds important, doesn't it? But I was only one of many on the staff. When I worked with various agencies and departments, however, I was treated as an important player because of the reference to the Governor's Office.

One day I was sitting in the visitor's section during the monthly meeting of a State agency when the members needed information about a piece of pending legislation to continue their discussion. I indicated to the chairman that I could help because, as part of my responsibilities, I was monitoring that particular legislation.

He invited me to sit in a vacant chair at the board table to contribute to the deliberation. When the discussion ended, I stayed seated at the table. No ulterior motive, I just did it. No one told me to move. At the next monthly meeting, I again sat in that same chair. This time there was an ulterior motive. I wanted to see if anyone would tell me to move. No one did. After all, I was from the Office of the Governor! Perceived Power.

For the record, my curiosity was satisfied, so I never sat there again.

These are interesting illustrations showing that most people don't want to say, "No." They are reluctant to ask for credentials or proof of identity. Because someone plays a role, others follow without question. This happens in political settings where Regulations are developed to explain how legislation is to be implemented. Elected officials with authority write legislation, but unelected bureaucrats write regulations. Although intended to be help-

ful, the regulations often become more stringent and restrictive than the legislation ever intended.

I asked a former colleague of mine, a regulation
writer, why he wrote such restrictive requirements when
he had absolutely no legal authority to do so. With all se-
riousness, he answered, "That's what the legislation
should have said!" That was the height of presumption
and arrogance without authority.

In our business and personal lives, we are required
and expected to follow legal and reasonable rules, but we
must be careful to assure those rules come from authorized parties. We should guard against accepting something simply because someone with *perceived power* says
so.

If unsure, ask questions. Say, "No," and don't let the
playing field be "leveled" just because it seems like a
good idea at the moment. Check for implications and
consequences.

Building a Kitchen Cabinet

Many businesses today include a kitchen cabinet in
their corporate structure because of its value. This kitchen
cabinet, however, has nothing whatsoever to do with the
employee break room – as important as that is for morale
and productivity. This one contributes a great deal to
company communication, business growth, and personal
development.

The idea of a kitchen cabinet is an interesting play on
words, and it relates specifically to management as well
as the sharing of ideas and opinions. The play on words
refers to the formal and official advisory body of the
President of the United States – the Cabinet – the group

appointed to advise the president on all issues related to governing the country. In most instances it works well, but there have been exceptions to that smooth advisory function.

Because he disliked and distrusted the members of his official advisory body, President Andrew Jackson gathered a group of trusted friends to serve as his advisors and ignored the "official" cabinet. This unofficial advisory group often met at the White House – in the kitchen – thus the "Kitchen Cabinet" was born.

In later years, both John F. Kennedy and Ronald Reagan relied upon and valued the same type of trusted advisors. It also shows the concept has no political party affiliation, preference, or bias. Regardless of party preference, all presidents seek advice and counsel from trusted associates.

In business, although cabinet positions, per se, don't exist, there are scores of staff members such as department heads, directors, and other managers who are the official advisors to upper level management. Many senior executives also have their personal, but unofficial, trusted advisors.

Even though there isn't a solid-line relationship displayed on the corporate organizational chart those kitchen cabinet members have direct contact with "the boss," and information and communication between them flow freely, quickly, and constantly. It behooves everyone to recognize the existence of the Kitchen Cabinet and the valuable role it can play.

Not too long ago in this section, we discussed the impact of "Perceived Power" in which individuals were accorded deference and obedience because they were *thought* to have power in an organization In many respects, the Kitchen Cabinet is the direct opposite of that concept. Specific individuals are not seen as powerful or influential, but in fact they are! They are part of an inner circle, and their contacts with the real authority are constant although not visible to many other employees. They can "get things done" because the formal structure and organization don't hinder communication and influence.

Creating and maintaining a Kitchen Cabinet can be a valuable management tool in business because it enables executives to get advice, reactions, and feedback in a way that is flexible and easy to maneuver. The "meetings" of a kitchen cabinet almost never convene at the workplace. They are informal, often at the boss's home as part of other social activities. Of course, no minutes are taken and "Robert's Rules of Order" are not followed.

Conversations and discussions are often heated as members express diverse points of view. The informality of the setting encourages openness and diversity of thought and expression, and because it is a meeting of "equals" everyone's ideas are encouraged, solicited, and valued. No one "wins" or "looses." Decisions are made on the basis of the freewheeling exchanges.

It might be well worth considering how such an advisory group can work within your organization. Certainly, it's a far cry from a formal and traditional managerial style, but plenty of evidence exists that testifies to the value.

Formal office settings can stifle the exchange of ideas, but the social environment of the kitchen can open and encourage dialogue.

I suggest you consider building a Kitchen Cabinet, and see what happens. Even if it ultimately doesn't work for you, at least you will have developed some close personal relationships, as well as a chance to taste new foods, drinks, and deserts.

That's not all bad.

Follow the Leader

Visual messages can overpower words every time. Here's what I'm getting at. A while ago I was visiting a friend who was president of a rather large marketing company. We met in his office late in the afternoon. As I was leaving after the meeting he told me he planned to stay for a while longer because he had some work to finish up. And besides that, he told me he simply liked to work late. He joked about this saying, "I come in so early, I have to make up for it by staying late."

On the way out, I noticed many of his staff were still there, too, even though it was well after what most of us would consider regular working hours. "Great dedication to the job," I thought as I left.

A few weeks later I was at a meeting with one of my friend's direct reports – people who report to the superior – and I happened to comment on seeing him and many of his colleagues in the office so late. When I mentioned their strong work ethic, he smiled and said, "It's because Charlie always stays so late. We have to pass his office on the way out, and most of us don't want him to see us leave while he's still at his desk. So we stay around, too. Makes it tough at home sometimes, but that's part of the job."

Charlie was sending a message he never intended to send.

I later told that to Charlie, without names of course, and a short while later he started to do something I thought was interesting, creative, and effective. (Subtle, too). At about 5:20 p.m. he turned out the lights in his office and left the building. No one knew it, but all he did then was go for a long walk, read the paper again over a cup of coffee, and then return to the office about 6:30 p.m. Everyone was gone by then, and he went back to work for a while because he truly did like working late.

The second event is similar, and it involves using technology. For many personal reasons, a colleague of mine, Sheri is her name, chose to deal with her voluminous e-mail messages on Sunday afternoon.

It fit her schedule, and she was able to carve out sufficient time to respond to simple inquiries as well as "emergencies."

No one was in the office when she decided to work there and, of course, she could work in private at home.

After this went on for many weeks, a confidant of hers shared some tension that was developing in her department. Many of her direct reports began to pay attention to the Sunday work and felt a bit intimidated into thinking they were expected to work on Sunday too. Pressure was developing.

Now here is the tie in between the two events. In each one, the visual message was the strong one. Charlie never told, suggested, or even hinted he expected his staff to work as late as he did. He simply elected to do it himself because he liked it. It fit his life style.

It never dawned on him that his behavior was having such an impact on everyone else. Similarly, my weekend e-mailing friend chose her schedule because it was convenient for her. She never considered the effect she was having on others.

In both events, though, the behaviors overpowered the words. Charlie adjusted his work schedule at the end of his day. Sheri still types her e-mails on Sunday, but she doesn't hit the send button until Monday. Both modifications were easy, and both had significant and long term impacts on their respective staffs.

I suggest it might be a good idea if all of us carefully examine some of our activities in light of when and where they take place. It might be valuable for each of us to make an effort to really "see" what we are doing, rather than just "looking" at it.

The differences might be very important to us, to our customers, and to our colleagues.

CHAPTER 3

Message Clarity

Do all the work necessary to make messages clear. Don't expect an audience to work to understand you. They won't! That's your job. All messages are for someone other than the one sending them. In a single sentence: It's always about the audience.

In order to be effective and clear it's necessary to focus on your target audience and do what is necessary for them, not just comfortable for you.

Using the correct tactics has always been important, but with increasing international communication, mediated techniques, and multiple generations in the workforce, accuracy is absolutely essential.

This section illustrates how to construct strong messages and demonstrates what can go wrong. Simple structural techniques are described. Using them results in speed, focus, and brevity. You'll see examples of how to start, how to develop, and how to conclude messages in a wide range of media.

It's then up to you to do it and make it your own.

Old habits die hard, but these examples will make focusing easier and more effective while maintaining individual style. You won't find any "one style fits all" formulas because there isn't one. The emphasis throughout is on saying what you mean and not having to repeat and correct. That just uses up time and material.

Wishful Thinking Isn't Goal Setting.

Many, if not all, companies have a goal statement. It might be prominently displayed near the reception area, or it might be printed on corporate stationery. Look around, and you'll find it.

A problem with many such statements, however, is they are interchangeable from company to company. Each one focuses on being the "best," the "first," the "strongest," the "most profitable," and "offering the highest level of customer service." There are more, of course, but these will make the point.

They all sound good, but they omit two important elements: *when* and *how*. Without answers to those two questions, Corporate Goal Statements or Mission Statements are simply Wishful Thinking. They don't specify directions or limitations. Without limitations or directions there will be no sense of urgency, no progress reports, and no assessment about "how we're doin'."

Here's a powerful example of goal setting at the highest Federal level. When President Kennedy addressed a Special Session of Congress in May, 1961, he said, "I believe that this nation should commit itself to achieving the goal, before this decade is out, of landing a man on the moon and returning him safely to the earth."

The two necessary elements were clear. First, commitment of resources and, second, a timetable: the end of the decade. On July 21, 1969, Neal Armstrong and Buzz Aldrin stepped on the Moon – 8 years, 1 month, and 28 days after the president's speech. No wishful thinking there.

That's an extreme example, so let's look at goals and wishful thinking on other, more personal and business related level. We've all heard people talking about wanting to improve themselves by getting a better job, writing a book, or earning an MBA degree, or improving department productivity. All worthy and desirable activities, but each one requires effort and planning. As long as they remain just items on a "bucket list," they are only wishful thinking. When they remain on that list for a long time, they lead to disappointment because they probably won't happen.

By adding a few words, however, the wishes become plans. For example, how can you earn that MBA degree? You must enroll in an appropriate academic institution for a specific semester.

Get started. Take a course, and continue taking the necessary courses, until you earn the required number of credits. Depending on your other time commitments, that might take a while, but you'll eventually achieve the goal, not just think about it. You might also get the better job you want.

Review your personal and professional "bucket list." What must you do to reach your personal and corporate goals? Without answering the *what* and *how* questions there will be no focused activity. There might be busy-work but no progress.

Consider this advice of the Cheshire Cat in *Alice in Wonderland*. When Alice came to a fork in the road, she asked the Cat, "Which road do I take?"

The Cat said, "That depends a good deal on where you want to get to."

Alice responded, "I don't care where."

The Cat said, "Then it doesn't matter which way you go…"

"…so long as I get somewhere?" was her reply.

"Oh, you're sure to do that, if only you walk long enough," offered the Cat.

What impact could that advice have on you and your business? Following the Cheshire Cat's advice, silly as it might sound, can transform your wishful thinking into goal setting.

One more bit of advice from Lewis Carroll spoken by the King to the White Rabbit on how to get started. It certainly reflects our suggested action plan.

"Begin at the beginning, go until you come to the end, then stop.

Once you have an idea, a goal, do something about it and keep at it until you finish. Then wishful thinking becomes goal setting – and achievement.

Try it.

Judge a Book by Its Cover.

Since childhood we've been told, "Don't judge a book by its cover." Good advice, but most of us don't always follow it. We often make instantaneous judgments about people.

These visual stereotypes sometimes work for us, but this rush to judgment can produce problems. Most of us don't like to admit to stereotypes, but we all fall victim to them. Quickly, what kinds of people do the following passages describe?

A thin woman, wearing horn-rimmed glasses and a black dress with a high white collar.

A long-haired young, man wearing an earring and carrying a guitar.

An overweight, middle-aged man in a wrinkled suit, carrying an attaché case.

A tall, straight-backed young man with very short hair, shaved around the ears, wearing pressed cammies and highly polished boots.

Your first ideas were probably something like these: 1. A librarian or a teacher; 2. A rock musician or folk singer; 3. A salesman; and 4. A marine or a soldier. But the people described could be: 1. A wealthy art patron or a supreme court judge; 2. A teacher; 3. A foreign diplomat; and 4. A clothes model. You get the idea.

In our diverse business community, we have no way of knowing about the people who come into our workplaces. Most of us resist the temptation to make quick judgments. We're usually good at doing that, but the pressures of time and economics can combine, and we do judge the book by its cover.

The point is this. Costumes and appearances give impressions that have varied interpretations. That's what we have to consider.

Recently, there was an example of the visual stereotype when the Scottish lady, Susan Boyle, was a contestant on *Britain's Got Talent*. Her very plain appearance caused everyone to expect little of her. She was even ridiculed – until she began to sing! As they say, "The rest is history." She was wonderful. But, everyone had assumed the worst because the visual got in the way.

Here's another business example. Many years ago, a friend of mine, Paul, planned to purchase a new Mustang convertible. Wearing fringed cut-offs, a T-shirt, and gym shoes, Paul went into the dealership. No one paid any attention to him. In time, a salesman approached Paul and said, "Nice car isn't it, kid?"

Paul said, "Yes. It is."

The salesman said, "It's pretty expensive."

Paul said, "I suppose so."

"Probably a lot more than you can afford."

"Thanks, mister."

Paul headed toward the door, and the salesman returned to his associates. But Paul stopped short of the door, turned around, and walked back to the car. From the pocket of those fringed cut-offs, Paul extracted a large roll of hundred dollar bills.

The salesman came back as Paul counted out thirty-four hundred dollar bills on to the hood of the car. (Remember, this was a long time ago.) The price of the car was $3,400.

When Paul got to 34, the salesman's eyes popped, and he displayed a big smile, seeing a sale in the offing.

The smile disappeared quickly, though, as Paul picked up each hundred-dollar bill and returned the roll to the fringed cut-offs.

As the salesman watched, Paul said, "When I came in here, I intended to buy this car. But there's no way I'd ever buy a car from you."

The salesman sputtered, "But, but—"

Paul left and found another dealership.

In both these examples people judged those two "books by their covers," and they were wrong.

It serves all of us well to go beyond how a customer looks and to probe for content. When we resist the quick judgment there's no telling what might appear. The exploration might take a little extra time and patience, but the outcome can be dramatic.

Look at the book cover, but then be sure to read what's inside.

Where Is Your Message?

Sometimes a message comes from unexpected sources which might help you make your point. Or they might destroy it. You have to pay attention to all the details and remember the motto, "Whatever you do – do it on purpose."

Here's an interesting story about an unexpected message and it consequences. A few years ago, a business associate of mine (named Paul), an account executive at a Chicago advertising agency, worked with his company's creative team on a proposal for a new campaign for an airline. The contract would have been a significantly profitable agreement. The creative team worked hard to develop what turned out to be an exciting campaign – sure to secure a significant market share and income for the airline and profit for the advertising agency. I saw the storyboards and was privy to the focus of the campaign. It was great!

Paul arranged a date and time for the presentation to the airline management. When the scheduled date arrived, Paul and the creative team flew from Chicago to the airline's corporate headquarters. The "pitch" presentation was to take place in the Corporate Board Room – excellent for what they wanted to show to the management team. After setting up the materials for the presentation, they were ready with a terrific pitch which had been carefully edited and thoroughly rehearsed!

The airline executives arrived right on time. A good sign of their interest. After all the players introduced themselves to each other, Paul and his team were eager to begin, but they were told the airline CEO wanted to sit in on the presentation.

They were asked to delay the start for a few minutes and, of course, they agreed. Having the CEO in the audience would help make a decision. They would have the chance to talk directly to the most senior executive at the airline.

When the CEO arrived, he graciously greeted everyone on Paul's creative team. He shook hands with everyone and thanked them for coming. He glanced at the storyboards and the other material and said again, "Thank you for coming." Then he said, "This meeting is over."

With that he walked out of the room. Everyone was dumbfounded. No pitch had been made. No details had been explained. Nothing had been described. Because the meeting was over, they wouldn't have an opportunity to pitch anything. All the other airline executives exited the room, leaving Paul and the others asking each other, "What just happened?"

Then one of the team members saw the problem. United Airlines baggage tags were clearly visible on the cases they had used to carry their material from Chicago. As the CEO had glanced at the presentation materials, he saw they had all flown to the meeting on a competitive airline. Not a smart move!

The CEO's position was clear. Although unspoken, he told them, "If you want to represent my airline, fly on my planes." They could have flown on that airline, but old habits in the travel office never considered that option. United Airlines was always the first choice since it is a Chicago based company. The result of that decision was devastating. Paul and his colleagues didn't have a chance to explain their campaign concepts that day. And they never got back for a second chance. The United Airlines baggage tags spoke volumes to the CEO, and they sent a message far more powerful than anything the team had planned to say. Those few pieces of paper had overpowered their creative message. All the effort, all the time, all the travel, all the creativity went for naught.

Paul and his colleagues never returned to that airline. All their work and ideas were lost because they hadn't thought of a small but critical detail. Those baggage tags were the message at that meeting. Nothing else even came close. In an instant, those tags destroyed all the chances to deliver the intended and carefully rehearsed message about the proposed advertising campaign. An avoidable oversight led to a great waste and a lost opportunity, but that oversight was *The* message.

"Small Stuff" Counts.

How we interact with others is a matter of perspective, focus, and attitude. The choices we make determine how we behave in many situations.

Most of us have heard these directions: Look at the big picture. Use the 10,000-foot perspective. Take a bird's eye view. Reflect a global perspective.

And, we've often been told to concentrate on the overview and not get caught up in details. However, in 1999, Richard Carlson, Ph.D., published an interesting book titled, *Don't Sweat the Small Stuff...and It's All Small Stuff*. In fact, he published a series of *Don't Sweat...* books. All were very successful and popular. Good reading! Thoughtful. Provocative!

Without disputing Dr. Carlson's position, I'd like to suggest an alternative approach. Here's mine: In every aspect of daily life, "You better sweat the small stuff because all big things are made from small stuff."

Consider this: The U.S. Constitution is collection of a few basic ideas. The Sahara Desert is nothing more than a collection of grains of sand. A tsunami consists of multiple drops of water. A symphony is just a lot of musical notes. The Space Station is a combination of thousands of parts. A cathedral is an accumulation of stones. *Hamlet* is a collection of single words. A motion picture consists of thousands of still pictures. Your company is a group of individual people.

Big things are only a collection of small stuff. We can do something about small stuff, and our actions then have an impact on the big things. A simple example: It's easy to put out a campfire, but it's hard to fight a forest fire.

If we don't pay attention to the small stuff in business, the accumulation might consume us. Just what are those small items that require our attention? Here is a partial list in no particular order. A valuable product, a fair price, product reliability, pleasant work force, inviting surroundings, helpful employees, consistency, interest, a smile. Add your own.

So, let's look at small things all around us – things we can control and adjust – and see what they can produce.

At the start of any business venture all we have is an idea, a desire, and hopefully, a plan. Next we get a customer, and we have an activity with a single participant. As we acquire additional customers, we eventually grow into a real business. The best way to do that is to treat every person with the special care and attention he or she deserves and expects. The positive word of mouth advertising that comes with such customer service converts each small activity into a valuable business relationship. If we don't take care of each customer, however, that growth will slow, shrink, and die.

In a separate section, I wrote about how the principles in the Boy Scout Law make a good manager. Those same principles apply here. Each, in itself, is small, but collectively, the impact is immense. Every one of us has the capacity to control and develop the little things in our business. When we do that, the big picture comes into focus. Clearly, we control our own destiny.

Here's a final thought on "small stuff." The Art Institute of Chicago contains an excellent example of how "little things" create a "big thing." I'm referring, of course, to the masterpiece painted by Georges Seurat. *A Sunday Afternoon on the Island of La Grande Jatte* is made up of thousands of tiny dots. The style is called "Pointillism" in which the dots, according to Webster's "optical unification," form a single hue in the viewer's eye, which is more brilliant and powerful than brush strokes. The painting is approximately 7 feet by 10 feet (6'8" x 10'10" to be exact).

That's a lot of dots, and those small dots combine to create the total painting. Seurat certainly found it necessary to "...sweat the small stuff." Anyone who has seen the painting is glad he took the time to create this work.

And it will work for our businesses, too.

Is It Really "Policy"?

In many business settings, employees often use a sentence that can either lead to concluding a discussion and/or conversation, or produce a conflict and a confrontation. That sentence is, "It is our policy to _____." Employees often use it with colleagues, and, more importantly, with customers.

I'm not going to minimize the importance of having company policy clearly written for the benefit of employees and customers. And, in many respects, the larger the company, the more important is it to have clearly written policies.

What I want to caution, however, is the habit of using the sentence when such a policy might not actually exist. All of us should be aware of the difference between corporate policy and common practice. And we should be sure every one of our employees knows the difference in order to avoid possible conflicts with customers.

A couple of brief definitions are in order.

In business settings, "Policy" is a formal decision made and agreed to by management on how elements of a business will be implemented. The statements are specific and are included in some formal publication such as a policy manual, corporate minutes, or an employee handbook.

"Practice," on the other hand, reflects the way things have been done in the past. They are behaviors that have become commonplace and habitual. They are informal and aren't usually in print, so they are often subject to broad and, sometimes, convenient interpretations.

Here's an example of why understanding the difference between "policy" and "practice" is so important. This event happened recently in a major retail department store, and a simple transaction turned into a major confrontation.

A customer was purchasing an item as a gift and asked the clerk to mail it out of state.

So far, simple.

When the clerk totaled the cost, she included the state sales tax, and the customer reminded her that no sales tax should be considered because the item was being mailed to a state that had no sales tax.

That, indeed, was true at that location at the time of the purchase.

There was a brief exchange of the "Yes it is/no it isn't" variety between clerk and customer. Such exchanges, of course, never go anywhere.

The clerk finally announced quite strongly, "We charge the sales tax. That's our policy."

The red flag went up for the customer! The situation wasn't quite so simple any more. The customer then said, "If that's your company policy, show it to me. If it's policy, it's written down somewhere."

When the clerk couldn't produce the policy, she called her manager for help.

The manager also quickly informed the customer it was company "policy," but he couldn't produce it in writing either.

By now the conversation had grown louder, and a small group of other interested shoppers had gathered around to observe what had become a confrontation.

In time, the manager authorized the sale without the tax. The customer paid and left, saying she would never shop in the store again.

I have no way of knowing if she ever did return, but at the moment she made the comment, she was angry enough to keep that promise.

A customer relationship had been jeopardized because of a "policy" that no one could find. It was the practice of the store to charge the sales tax, and as far as the clerk and the manager were concerned, that was how it was done.

Their quick use of the word "policy," and their inability to produce it when challenged, resulted in losing at least one customer, maybe more.

That's a pretty high price to pay for choosing an incorrect word. The "takeaway" here is this. Be sure all of your employees know the difference between "policy" and "practice."

Many employees are tempted to use the work "policy" because it sounds strong, puts them in a power position, and often intimidates customers.

It might conclude a conversation, but if a customer demands documentation, the clerk will lose credibility, and the company may suffer the loss of a customer.

Make sure an inaccurate word doesn't provoke a costly confrontation. It isn't worth it.

Speed or Clarity?
Do You Have to Pick One Over the Other?

Newspaper editors and book publishers are very conscious of how their publications look. The newspapers you read have a clearly identifiable appearance. The page layout and type font and size are all designed to increase readership and help readers navigate through the paper. From time to time, the "look" of a newspaper is changed, and every modification is designed to make it easier for readers to get information.

Book publishers, likewise, select type styles to fit the text and invite readers to flow through the book. I recently looked at the books I have had published, and it was interesting to see how different each looked from the others. Different editors and different publishers had very different perceptions of what would work best for each book.

It seems appropriate for us in various businesses to follow the lead of the print professionals when we produce words on paper or on screen. Regardless of our specific product or service, we are all in the communications business so we should apply the best strategies. The main lesson from the print professionals is to make it easy for readers to find and understand information. The focus must be on the needs of the readers, not on the convenience or whim of the writer.

Here are two examples of writing I've seen over the years which are more favorable to the writer than to the reader. I'm sure you can add many more.

Let's look at e-mail first. One of the main advantages of e-mail is speed. Another is convenience. That speed and convenience, however, are usually for the benefit of the writer and, often, they make the end product difficult for the reader to understand.

Just before I began writing this section I worked my way through an e-mail, and the word "worked" is the important one here. Because of the sender's name and the subject line, I knew I had to read the message. It was difficult, though, because of the "distinctive" font the writer had selected. Knowing the writer as I do, I knew he wanted his e-mail to "stand out" and to look different from other e-mail messages. He certainly succeeded in making it look different with the font and size he had selected, but that difference got in the way of his intended message. What was convenient for him made it almost impossible for me and the others on his distribution list to understand him. What's the point of doing that?

Now a brief look at a paper message. I received a long, detailed memo from a business associate and the entire page was covered with tiny type, single-spaced with very narrow margins. Again, I waded through it because I assumed it was going to be important. When I saw him recently I asked why he had used such a small font. His answer was a surprise. His company has a requirement of writing only one-page memos, and he had adhered to that practice. He told me, though, he had so much to cover it would have been impossible to get everything on one page if he used the usual 10 or 12 point font.

"If I didn't use that small size, I could never get all the information on a single page," was his reasoning. He had followed the letter of the requirement, but he missed the spirit of the "one-page" idea. What's the point of that?

We all write in a variety of media every day, so be sure to place the needs and ease of the reader before your own convenience. Take a few extra minutes of your time as you write. Design and execute your material clearly so your readers won't have to use more of their time to figure out what you're telling them. Such considerate use of your reader's time will demonstrate your respect for your readers, and that respect will contribute to building and strengthening the relationships so important in business.

Do You Communicate or Do You Transmit?

Businesses give a great deal of lip service to the importance of communication. Managers often give speeches about it to their employees and customers. Employees and customers listen and nod their heads. Sometimes they even shake their heads.

That's the problem. The employees and customers are present, but often that's the extent of their active participation. Corporate information usually flows from the top down. Memos, policies, rules, regulations, and decisions originate from "on high," and those who receive that information are expected to comply. Certainly there are many instances when this chain-of-command is appropriate. Someone has to give the marching orders and set the direction, or chaos results. When it is necessary for you as a business leader to give specific directions, by all means, do so. In previous sections I used the line "Whatever you do, do it on purpose." It applies here.

Whenever you have to tell or direct, do it, but that's

not communication. That's transmission. Communication, by definition is a closed system, a loop. It requires that information travels full circle. First from a speaker to a listener, then the roles reverse, and the initial listener becomes the speaker while the speaker becomes the listener. This role reversal allows everyone to participate equally in the process.

Now, here's an interesting point. Each of the participants plays a variety of roles in the communication process. Speaker number one must first select an appropriate code in order to send his message (words, gestures, symbols, etc.), because we don't yet know how to send out thought waves. The receiver must understand the code, or the message dies. Next he must determine what he thinks the decoded message means. In other words, he interprets the message. And that interpretation is based on all of the factors that make him a unique individual: age, gender, experience, etc.

This is the point where the role reversal takes place. Now the initial receiver encodes a new message based on his interpretation and sends it to the other party who decodes and interprets it and then encodes yet another message. That's communication, and it's based on two or more parties being equally involved and playing both roles.

In order for true communication to occur, a speaker crafts his message based on his knowledge of the intended receiver. He considers what words, gestures, symbols, etc. will be understood by the receiver and how they will be interpreted. To be effective, a speaker must first think of and understand his audience. He must consider who they are and what they want, need, know, expect, require, etc. If a speaker doesn't know his audience, his customers, he runs the possibility of sending the wrong message.

Here is an example. A while ago I tracked the focus

of the CEO of a Midwest based transportation company. He said, "From now on, the focus of this company will be the customer, the customer, the customer." Sounded good. A few months later, as he described potential changes to address company problems, he said, "People think of our airline when they fly overseas, but probably don't make it their first choice for traveling to tourist getaways." That kind of comment suggested he might not have a good fix on his customers. Who did he think filled up all his company's airplanes bound for Orlando, Florida? Later he said, "There are four groups of people who must be convinced concerning this new strategy: stakeholders, bankers, employees, and the capital markets."

There was no reference to, "the customer, the customer, the customer." We'll wait to see what his plan is, and if it works.

More importantly for us here, however, is to consider how we craft and distribute our information. We recognize that it's easy to just send out messages, but it's also important to determine if those messages are received and understood.

Such understanding comes from effective communication, not from transmission.

Every Decision Is Forever.

Every decision you make is based on the set of conditions that exist at the moment you make it. Once made, you can't go back. Conditions are different now from what they were only moments earlier. Of course, you may make a new, different, or revised decision, but the factors are no longer exactly the same. So use care and select cautiously because you are affecting the rest of your life and the lives of others around you every time you make a decision.

One of my favorite poems is, "The Road Not Taken" by Robert Frost. In the poem he describes a man walking in the woods. When the man comes to a fork in the road he must choose one path or the other. Both paths looked about the same, except one seemed to be a little less traveled. He made his choice, knowing he could never come back to that exact spot again. He was comfortable with his selection, and he knew choosing one over the other "...made all the difference." If you haven't read the poem, or if it has been some time since you read it, allow me to suggest you find a copy, read it, and reflect on how it relates to your business behavior.

What does this poem have to do with business and, specifically with business communication? Everything you say and do during the day affects other people and changes the conditions in which they live and work. These changes aren't necessarily earth shattering, but they do make differences, which we should recognize.

Here are a couple of brief examples. The first is pure fiction, but the second was an actual event.

In the first example, an employee came into your office with a request to leave early that afternoon. You were under pressure and working under a tight timetable so you quickly said "No." You made a decision, but the relationship between you and your employee changed from what it was only moments earlier. There may now be disappointment, anger, frustration, or worry. Then the employee continued to talk, saying, "But my son was just taken to the hospital." What would you say now? Probably you would now say, "Yes." But the relationship between the two of you has already changed a bit.

All you had to do was ask for information before making that first decision. Then you would have been seen as understanding, caring, and involved rather than pressured, quick, and insensitive. Big difference.

Before you make a comment to anyone, consider how it might be received because as soon as you deliver a message the conditions and the relationships change. And they'll never go back to being exactly where they were before you acted. So ask yourself this question: Will the new condition be better or worse than the previous one?

Here's the second example – the actual one. I know of an instance in which a store clerk walked right past a customer without asking if he could help, without even acknowledging the customer was there. Obviously that wasn't good customer service in this particular business which prided itself on such service, but was it a significant decision?

In this case it certainly was. The "customer" was the new CEO of the company and was very displeased with the extremely poor customer service. The CEO asked the store manager if he might use his office phone and, with the manager standing there, he called the president of the company to describe what had just happened. Needless to say, no one was happy. Changes were made in that store and throughout the company after that brief, but significant, encounter.

That clerk had a choice to make, to help or to walk on by. He made his decision, and as Robert Frost wrote, "That has made all the difference" in the clerk's employment, in the manager's status, and in the customer service training and delivery in that chain of stores.

Certainly, this is just a single instance, but it reflects the challenges and opportunities we all face every day as we work with and communicate with those around us. Each decision is important, each one makes all the difference, and each one lives forever!

Hard-to-Believe Comments

A few years ago, the chief executive of an engineering organization was asked what impact removing sand from a barrier island sandbar would have on the beach. With great self-assurance and a deep strong voice, he said, "There will be absolutely no damage, but if there is any, it won't be very much."

An examination of that sentence makes it clear he had no idea what damage might occur. He sounded good, but his comment made no sense. With increasing frequency, thanks to expanding communication media, we're seeing and hearing many such "sounds good – means nothing" statements, making it essential for all of us to carefully process messages.

Anyone who has ever cast a vote on any matter knows why the following sentence sounds so strange. I'm sure you'll remember it. "We have to pass this bill so we can find out what's in it." That's backward!

On the other side, here's one that sounds strange but actually makes sense. You'll remember this one too. "I voted for it before I voted against it." Much was said about that, but it makes sense when we recognize that people change their minds about issues. When new information becomes available, positions change. To remain rigid in the face of new information is arrogant. But that sentence still sounds strange – even comical.

These examples are from live press conferences where immediate responses to questions were necessary. Under pressure, speakers might select inappropriate words. Certainly, the examples demonstrate that. What's even more significant, however, is when advertising or promotional copy presents seemingly contradictory information. As comments move to print, more than one person is involved in the process. Writers, editors, proofreaders, etc. all have a chance and a responsibility to identify and correct errors. Because of all the checkpoints, errors are even more serious and sometimes much funnier.

Here are some I've collected over the years. I've used some of them before, but in this day and age of language misuse, they are worth repeating. Maybe you can add to my list.

At the pharmacy counter of a major drug store chain this sign was prominently displayed, "Flu shots – given while you wait." Of course! The pharmacist can't e-mail the shot to you or deliver it by overnight carrier.

A cultural center advertised a new offer this way, "The exhibit is free with paid admission." Seems to be something missing here.

In its television advertising, a major tire company offers this incentive. "Buy 2 tires, get 2 free. Buy 3 tires, get 1 free." That one is really hard to interpret. It probably has something to do with different brands, but it certainly looks and sounds strange and confusing – and wrong.

Here's another "wrong" comment we mentioned earlier and often hear in business and political circles. "Walk the walk, and talk the talk." The comment is intended to indicate focus, strength, and commitment, but it doesn't. The correct comment is "Walk the talk." That describes someone who has the courage to do what he says he'll do. It makes sense, and it demonstrates confidence. "Walk the talk" is a contemporary version of, "Put your money where your mouth is," but it's a bit gentler.

Sometimes the source of an erroneous statement multiplies the severity of the mistake. Here's one from a United States Senator. "The three branches of the US government include the President, the Senate, and the House of Representatives." A moment of research anywhere will list the three branches as Executive, Legislative, and Judicial. How could a U.S. Senator misplace an entire branch of government?

The lesson is clear. With every message you send, business and personal, take time to be sure it's accurate. People won't remember the medium we use, but they'll remember what we say.

High-speed media can be dangerous because they transmit messages faster than we can clarify them and, once spoken, our words can't be retrieved. They can live forever.

That's a sobering thought.

Too Much Information

Have you ever received an unsolicited ten-page letter from a stranger? I have, too. Did you take the time to read it? I didn't either.

During the past couple of weeks I received three such letters: one from an academic institution, one from a political organization, and one from a charitable foundation.

They all had serious messages to deliver and, in their eyes, everything was very important. But I can't figure out why anyone would expect a recipient to read all that verbiage just because it arrived in the mailbox. In the "good old days," whenever they were, people might have taken the time to read such lengthy letters but, today, with the e-mail mentality of the general population, that's asking the impossible – at least the improbable.

If and when you elect to or are charged with writing a form letter to customers, clients, contributors, or constituents, how can you do it quickly and effectively?

We've all heard the caution, "Keep it simple." Do it. It works. Easy to say, but precisely, how do you do that?

Try this.

First accept the fact that you don't have to include everything you know. Most of your readers won't want to know all of that, anyway. They don't want to and won't spend time wading through all those words. You may think everything is equally interesting, but what you write isn't for you – it's for your readers. So, pick just one or two major points, and develop each one. You can always write other volumes of details at a later time.

Once you know what you want to say – say it. Don't make your reader work to find your message. It isn't the reader's job to figure out what you want him to know. It's yours. Make your point right away, within the first paragraph. If possible, make it in the first sentence. That's Part One of this approach. It's the *What* of your letter.

As soon as the reader understands that, he's going to want to know *Why*, especially if your message is bad news. This is Part Two of the sequence. It's the background or justification for the letter.

When you have stated your message clearly, the background information makes sense. Unfortunately, many writers begin with the background. They intend to "set the stage," but the reader quickly asks himself, "What's this all about? Where's it going?" This background describes why you are sending the message, and it shouldn't precede the message.

Once you've stated what you want or need and why you want or need it, it's time for Part Three, which describes *How* you want it to be done.

Using this three-part sequence will make it easier for you to write the letter because your material is organized. That organization also will make it easier for your readers to understand and follow your train of thought. The process will encourage your readers to continue reading because your sequence makes sense. The logical flow will also keep you on track and avoid unnecessary detail.

Now, if you think the reader might want more details, put them in a clearly identified appendix. Note the availability, but don't force the reader to plow thought the entire message. Let the reader make the choice – don't make it a requirement. Just make your point, back it up, and move on.

Here's an additional assist to establishing the sequence. Think about time. Begin with what you want now, support it by describing what occurred before now, and develop the flow by describing what events or actions will happen after now. When you make it easy for a reader to follow your thoughts, he will, even if he doesn't agree with them. If you make it difficult to plow through your material, he won't. If your material isn't read, you've wasted your time, and the reader certainly won't bother to waste his.

Could I write more about this? Yes! Will I? Nope! I think I made my point.

Cancel That Meeting.

No matter the size of a company, a major activity is "meeting." From the top floor corner office to the basement storage room, everybody goes to meetings. "Going to a meeting" is part of the vocabulary of most workers, so let's ask this deeply penetrating question. "Why?"

Most of us go to meetings because it's "Monday at 9:00 a.m." (Feel free to insert your own time and day to make this segment relevant to your business.) Then because we have the time and the day, we have to figure out what to cover and include. We have to develop an agenda – or go through the same one we used at the previous meeting because most agendas aren't very creative or original. But, too often the real reason for the meeting is just the regular schedule, not the need for one. And with technology, virtual meetings often take place at very inconvenient times – many hours different from the initiating meeting location.

Meetings should be scheduled for need not predictability. Many organizations have evolved to a point where participants look forward to them because, at a meeting, they can "multi-task" and get e-mails and other work done while attending. In such situations, the participants are present in body but not in mind. Usually that's a colossal waste of time and resources.

If we look at meetings, we come to the realization there are – or should be – just two reasons to hold one: to *Learn* something or to *Do* something. Participants either acquire information and collect data or they resolve issues and solve problems. Both of those reasons require full attention and participation. That eliminates "multitasking" because, no matter how smart someone is, he or she cannot give 100% attention to more than one topic at the same time.

So if you are in a position to do so, cancel the "regularly scheduled meeting" until there is a good reason to hold it. Productivity will likely go up. If a meeting simply "provides information," that can easily be done via e-mail. Updates and status reports usually don't require discussion, but they can sure fill up a lot of time.

In regard to "action" meetings, I came across an interesting item recently that described the psychology of such a meeting. In all groups, one individual stands out as the "Leader." That's no surprise, but what usually happens is this. The Leader establishes a position and most of the others, the "Followers," either accept it without question or expand upon it. In real-time meetings, the Followers don't usually disagree openly with the Leader. The potential brainpower, therefore, doesn't get used in situations where discussions are necessary. There is little "give-and-take" debate, just agreement and acceptance.

To avoid that "top-down" pressure, here is an interesting option. Cancel the meeting, and ask each of the potential participants to send you hard copy or e-mail suggestions or recommendations about the topic you want to cover. With all of them in hand, review the input. It will be broader and more varied than would be the case in the typical meeting. Now you'll have more tools with which to make critical decisions, and collecting that varied information won't require participants to sit together at a specific time. This technique works because it unlocks a level of creative thinking in everyone, and it removes the intimidation many employees feel when they must take part in a group discussion. Writing responses provides time to think and freedom to explore ideas without fear of "feeling wrong." And that freedom results in what many describe as "thinking out of the box" when seeking solutions and planning action.

This certainly seems to be worth trying. Every work group is different, of course, but this option might be worth considering in order to broaden the spectrum of possibilities when seeking solutions to problems.

What do you think?

What Do You Think?

Have you ever called, or been invited to, a meeting where the agenda indicated something like, "developing a

solution to a problem?" At such meetings someone usually acts as a "facilitator" to gather and direct ideas and options. Sometimes "brainstorming" is the primary tactic, or
it might simply be an open discussion where an idea is
suggested, reviewed, revised, expanded, or constructed.
Most of the time the results are acceptable, and good ideas and suggestions can, and do, grow from such meetings.

There is a significant potential problem with this
technique, however, and it's worth noting. Let's assume
for now that everyone understands the reason for the
meeting – not just the agenda, but *Why* the meeting is going to take place and *What* should be accomplished.

The first shortfall stems from the participants themselves. Someone, usually the "senior person" is the "driver." That's the one who is most vocal, the one who always seems to be the first one to offer an idea. Most of
the other meeting participants are: "yes – but's," "ad-
ders," "expanders," or "refiners." They are the ones who
reframe the initial idea. These people rarely introduce
new ideas. They simply respond to the suggestions of the
"driver."

That process is popular, but something is lacking,
and it can be costly to an organization. It's easy to see
how the "driver" sets the tone and the direction of a conversation. With the "driver" in control, others hesitate to
introduce new or different ideas. Here's an example.

Driver says, "I think we should go to a movie." Others discuss: title, location, time, theater, competing titles,
etc., etc. Eventually, they'll work out the logistics, but the
certainty is they will go to a movie! The driver set the
direction.

In this type of meeting others hesitate saying, "That's
a possibility, but I think we should go to the Museum of
Art to see the new exhibit." Suggesting a totally different
idea would result in a discussion and decision-making

process quite unlike the driver-led meeting. It's difficult, however, to elicit that independent thinking, so how can we encourage it? Here's a suggestion.

Before a meeting, announce – clearly – its purpose. Make it specific and action oriented. Write it down, send it to every potential attendee. Here's the reason for writing. If you can't write it on a blank screen or piece of paper, the purpose is not clear in your own mind. If it isn't clear to you, how can anyone be expected to respond?

Have each attendee write what he or she believes will best address the issue. Again, writing the response will require the respondent to be specific and action-oriented. Have everyone send you the response before the meeting. The attendees will then have options from which to choose. Each one will be seen as equally likely and possible. The ensuing discussion will be on the merits of all the ideas rather than on the fine-tuning of a single "driver" suggestion. The value of the ideas will lead to a decision, not the personality or preference of the driver.

This process allows all ideas to be explored fully rather than agreeing or disagreeing with a single stated position. It also eliminates direct confrontation that usually leads to reluctant agreement.

It's a sad commentary because such behavior clearly states, "I really don't want to do this, but I'll go along with it for now." That avoids an immediate battle, but an entire war could be lost.

In government circles today such a decision is called, "Kick the Can." That's the name of a children's game many of us played years ago.

Such decisions in business and government have had powerful negative effects because participants were reluctant to offer alternatives, defend conflicting positions, or to simply say, "No."

This suggested alternative approach, relying on independent written recommendations, could have powerful positive implications when seeking solutions to issues we face during our business days.

CHAPTER 4

Language Usage

We live and work in a multi-lingual environment, but, for most of us, the language of business is American English. Most people think they're pretty good with it, but often what they think isn't so. Errors are abundant, and those errors can hurt an otherwise sound business image. People judge others by the language they use. That might be unfair, but it's what happens.

The skills and rules and techniques we all learned in school are often forgotten – or ignored – as we get older. We make excuses, and we ingrain habits that might be limiting. We become careless, and we make excuses for the mistakes, but other people remember them.

The following section serves as a reminder of what we should do and how we should do it. Some of the stories are humorous, but we don't want to be the cause of the humor – to be laughed at. That's not good for most businesses.

Many times we know what we do wrong, but we do it anyway.

That's always a bad idea!

Paradise In Wonderland

When Lewis Carroll wrote *Alice in Wonderland* and *Through the Looking Glass*, I'm sure his primary objective wasn't to provide lessons on effective business communications. However, there is a great deal of information on that topic in his tales. Recently, I reread Lewis Carroll and was struck by how some of his ideas fit so closely with our responsibilities in business. Let's look at a couple of scenes and reflect on their application to effective business communication. I'm sure you'll remember them.

We've all been faced with the need to make a presentation to management, customers, or clients. Perhaps the most difficult parts of carrying out such an assignment are deciding on an appropriate sequence, getting started, and getting to the "punch line." Well, here's some help from *Wonderland*.

At the trial determining who stole the Queen's tarts, the King of Hearts tells the White Rabbit to read the evidence. The White Rabbit asks the King, "Where shall I begin, please, your Majesty?"

The King responds, "Begin at the beginning, go on until you come to the end, then stop."

Simple, brilliant. An excellent sequence to follow. *First*, have a compelling start to your presentation. How will you begin? Why should your audience listen to you? *Second,* decide precisely what is your point. Why are you giving this presentation? *Third,* What should happen after your presentation? What do you want your listeners to do next? When you've covered those three items, stop! An otherwise good presentation is often ruined when a speaker doesn't know when to stop talking.

Here's another business gem from Lewis Carroll. This one relates to planning, vision, and corporate direction. When Alice met the Cheshire Cat she asked timidly, "Would you tell me please which way I ought to walk from here?"

"That depends a great deal on where you want to get to," replied the Cat.

"I don't much care where," said Alice.

"Then it doesn't matter which way you walk." said the Cat.

"I just want to get somewhere," Alice added.

"Oh, you're sure to do that," said the Cat, "if you only walk long enough."

Again, simple and to the point. In business, if we don't know exactly what we want to accomplish it doesn't make any difference how we use our talents. Many business people spend a great deal of time "beating out brush fires," but they accomplish little.

They expend huge amounts of energy responding to immediate situations, but they miss achieving their ultimate goals. They react to symptoms rather than solve problems.

We all have to keep working toward goals and focusing on the tasks we feel are important. In these difficult economic times, if we coast along after reaching a degree of success, but our competitors continue to work hard and smart, we'll lose ground – and market share – very quickly.

The Queen of Hearts had some advice for Alice on that matter too. She said, "It takes all the running you can do just to keep in the same place. If you want to get somewhere else, you must run at least twice as fast as that."

Finally, we are all immersed in a world of words. Those words we speak or write are not meant for us. We already know what we want and what we mean. Our words, therefore, must clearly communicate our ideas to others. If they don't understand our words, we've wasted everyone's time. If we aren't careful with our words, our audiences might reflect Alice's comment after she read the poem, "Jabberwocky." She said, "It seems pretty. Somehow, it seems to fill my head with ideas – only I don't know exactly what they are!"

I suspect many of us have heard speeches which have led us to that same conclusion. I found rereading Lewis Carroll was both fun and profitable. I invite you to visit "Wonderland" again.

You might be surprised by what you find there.

A Short Visit to "Grammarland"

Recently, I was conducting a class on business communication, and a participant brought up what might be new trend in customer service. A similar idea had been suggested in an earlier MBA graduate class I was teaching so I suspect there might be something going on in the business world that could be worth considering. Like most "new" items, this one has both good and bad aspects to it.

The new trend relates to what is happening in large call centers. A call center representative can talk to only one customer at a time. That means this is a very labor-intensive business. It's easy to see how the ebb and flow of call volume can influence the size of the call center work force. With expanding use of the Internet, however, more customers are using e-mail and instant messaging to communicate with companies. Call center operators, likewise, are using this development to their advantage. With instant messaging, call center operators can now handle two, three, or four calls at the same time. They can carry on written conversations with many more people than was ever possible on the telephone. Communicating with four customers simultaneously can provide much faster service, which is what customers want.

That's the good news, but here's the bad news part to this trend. As some call centers have made this shift, they are realizing that many representatives who worked the phones well have difficulty writing well. Effective communication with clients is suffering. Being able to talk well and being able to write well require two totally different sets of skills. Further, the permanency of speech and writing are very different. If someone makes an error while speaking, the error is gone in an instant. If, however, someone makes an error in print, that error lives forever.

We all know that how we communicate in business reflects on us personally, and it reflects on our companies. Poor writing reflects poorly on every company that allows it. This difficulty with writing ability, of course, exists with customers as well as with the call center personnel, but companies can't do anything to control or improve the skills of their customers. They can and should, however, improve the skills of their work force because of the importance of the messages they are sending to customers.

Many call center operators are looking to develop writing classes for their representatives so they can effectively use instant messaging. These won't be "going back to school" remedial classes filled with grammar rules and memorization, but it's a chance to revisit some of the basic skills we all struggled with in the past. In many cases when we got out of school we stopped paying close attention to what we learned in English grammar class. Those old rules, however, still apply today. Whether or not we like to admit it, we are still judged by our writing skills. The companies we represent are also judged by what we do.

If you are in a position to do so, help your work force make a brief visit to "Grammarland." Encourage employees to pay attention once again to such things as: agreement of subject and predicate, antecedents of pronouns, number, gender, case, sentence fragments, and accurate punctuation. You might even find it helpful to provide this instruction by arranging classes. It could be good for the employees and good for the company.

In my writing classes I've seen how quickly participants remember what they once learned. This revisiting of past grammar studies doesn't take a long time, but it does take concentration and focus. A couple of days and appropriate exercises usually provide the desired results.

As business continues to shift to increasing use of e-mail and instant messaging, a review of the basics of English grammar can be very helpful. A brief visit to "Grammarland" can add a great deal to the efficiency and effectiveness of the staff as well as to the image of the company.

"It" Isn't Broken. People Are Abusing "It."

Often, when a system ceases to function correctly, it's easy to place the responsibility on the organization or the business and declare it to be "broken." But the fact of the matter is the institutions are fine. The problem rests with the actions of the people inside the institutions.

Remember, people do things, institutions don't. Institutions take the blame because the people inside an organization are usually hidden by complexities. Since identifying a specific target individual is so difficult, communication breaks down, and words are misdirected. So is the blame. If we pick the wrong words, it's easy to send an incorrect message. In business and civic settings, indeed in every daily setting, the words we select focus on how we observe, categorize, and react to situations.

With increasing frequency we're seeing repeated references about "broken" institutions. We are told almost daily the "Government is broken," "Wall Street is broken," "Health Care is broken," "the Financial system is broken," "School systems are broken," "Religions are broken." And that's just the start of a long list. Everything seems to be "broken" or, at best, close to breaking.

Every day the media are filled with such comments, but they're wrong. People do those things. People in government, Wall Street, finance, education, business, health care, and religion are causing the problems. They are abusing the tenants of the institutions they represent. Many of those people are creating confusion and misunderstanding by using excessive verbiage, by miscommunication. Often, many of their statements seem to come with expiration dates, which cause subsequent problems. Ideas and concepts are drowned in seas of paper, and verbal bulk has taken priority over clarity and focus. The words people use to communicate ideas and principles form the perceptions others hold, and their focus and intent are demonstrated by their words. Sometimes those words cause confusion.

Here's an example: The former powerful Speaker of the U.S. House of Representatives made a strange and disturbing comment when she said, "We have to pass this (health care) bill to find out what's in it." That's just backward.

Whether that comment was deliberate or accidental is irrelevant. The fact is she said it, but we expect elected officials to know what a bill contains before casting a vote. "Broken" institutions are straw men which people often use to implement personal agendas. It's easier – and safer – to criticize an institution that to confront an individual. Rather than blaming institutions, however, look at the behavior of the people involved and ask what core values they demonstrate by their actions.

Ask simple questions like these: What intensions are they demonstrating? Are the responsible parties consistently telling the truth? Are they doing what's necessary to preserve our business institutions? Are they taking the actions that truly "preserve, protect, and defend" the values and principles that define us and describe our priorities?

Those words in quotation marks are from the Oath of Office of the President of the United States. Similar words are included in the oath taken by everyone entering military service. They are a good example of how brevity can be powerful and clear. And clarity is essential to focus on the actions of people rather than the vagaries and complexities of institutions. Excessive verbiage produces confusion. Effective communication is necessary to "get to the point" because what a document says is far more important than how much it weighs.

It's interesting to ask why the recent health care bill required 2,000+ pages when the United States Constitution, including all the Amendments, requires only 26 pages in the copy I recently purchased. It's easy to point at an institution and declare it "broken," but it takes time and it requires effort to look at the responsible parties, their motives, their core values, and their ethics.

Those factors define individual behavior, and the behavior of the people involved is what we should evaluate when we examine and judge the functioning of an institution. Such an evaluation will determine the need for and the value of supporting or changing any institution – and the people running it.

Our institutions aren't broken, but many individuals are abusing them.

Pick the Appropriate Word.

Most of what we do, we do by habit. Often those habits are helpful because they save time and effort. For example, we don't have to think about how to walk or how to form specific letters when we write. We've developed habits, which make these tasks easy. Because those habits are so comfortable, however, they sometimes limit how we behave, and they limit our options.

I thought about this during a business writing class I was teaching recently when a participant asked a question about selecting "good" and "bad" words. What developed from that question was a discussion about determining why and how we pick specific words and phrases when we write and when we talk.

The basic agreement from that discussion was this: Rather than thinking in terms of "right-wrong" or "good-bad," it's more effective to think about "appropriate" words.

Further, thinking carefully about the reader or the listener we're addressing is what will help determine what is appropriate.

Remember, what we write or say isn't for us, it's for someone else. So be sure the messages accurately communicate what you intend.

Ask yourself, "What words will have the effect I want?" Many of us, however, don't ask that simple question.

We select words by habit, not by design. Here's something else that complicates the matter even more. The words we use when we write are often different from the words we use when we speak. Most of us use two very different vocabularies as we conduct business, one for speech and one for writing.

We're going to review some of those differences in a moment, but first we'll take a brief look at another habit, the use of "redundant speech" or overkill speech.

This, too, is a habit where we use too many words.

We think we're being precise, but we're simply repeating ourselves unintentionally. I'm not sure if we developed this habit because we thought the repetition sounded good or because we never gave it much thought.

Think about these words, all of which I collected from various business and media sources. I'm sure you'll see how unnecessary many of the descriptors are. Inventors often describe "new innovations" What other kind are there? How about "old antiques? There couldn't be any other kind, could there?

A bit of dialogue from an adventure movie, "We were surrounded on all sides." If you're surrounded, you're surrounded!

The word means on all sides. "The contemporary world of today" appeared in an ad for new communication technology.

No explanation necessary here.

"Assemble the pieces together" was included in the direction sheet for a child's toy. "Perfect circle" and "perfect square" often appear in speech and in writing. It's impossible to have an imperfect circle or an imperfect square. Either a figure is a circle or square, or it isn't.

Simple. End of discussion.

These aren't great errors, of course, but they are unnecessary words, and using them can cause a reader or listener to question our knowledge of the language. None of us wants to create such a question. That brings us back to the "good-bad" words and the use of appropriate words.

The words we select carry meaning about our ideas, but they also influence how our listeners and readers evaluate and react to us. Such evaluation is unfair, but everyone does it. It's in our best interest, then, to make careful choices.

Everyone will be familiar with every word included in the list below, but think about this.

The first word in each pair is the one we would most likely use when we write, and the second one is the way we talk.

The first word may be perfectly correct in particular situations, but the second one is more direct and less stilted.

Here is the selection of word pairs: achieve, do; commence, begin; contribute, give; finalize, finish; has the ability to, can; in the event that, if; parameters, limits; prioritize, rank; remuneration, payment; state of the art, latest; terminate, end.

There are many more like these, but I hope these pairs will get you thinking about other words you use, and why you use them. Business writing is usually more effective and clearer when we use the second word in the sample pairs. Listen carefully to the words you and your colleagues use and decide which are appropriate for specific situations.

Finally ask yourself, "Do the words I use create the result I want?"

Use Language for Clarity, Not Just Convenience.

"My eyes literally popped out of my head when I saw the budget projections!"

That's a frightening and visually revolting image! I heard a CEO make that statement recently, and it brought to mind how often I've heard such misuse of a word or phrase for the sake of emphasis or impact.

"Literally" means that's exactly what happened – a fact, a description of an event. That CEO's eyes didn't "pop out of his head." What he said was just wrong. What he intended was to make a point, to exaggerate, to create an impression. We hear it often. "I literally fell off my chair." "I literally flew up the stairs." Such actions didn't happen. No one fell and, certainly, no one flew. With increasing frequency, though, the word "literally" is being used for emphasis, but it's just wrong, and it shouldn't be used that way. It almost seems users want to impress listeners with the depth of their vocabulary. But does the misuse of "literally" show depth?

There are scores of other misused words to add to a list of verbal errors committed with the intent to emphasize or to impress. Look at these misuses: "a perfect circle." That doesn't make sense because it's impossible to have an imperfect circle. Either a figure is a circle, or it isn't. Same with a "perfect square." How about "almost exactly," or "most unique," or "more perfect," or "perfectest"? If we take just a moment to think about these words we see the modifiers are all unnecessary.

Either something is "exact," or it isn't. Same with "unique," which is defined as "having no equal" or "one and only." Something is unique, or it isn't. It's interesting to note, however, there are always exceptions to these rules, and you can get away with such misuse if you have enough status. In the Preamble to the United States Constitution, for example, James Madison, the primary author, referred to forming "a more perfect union," and no one corrected him. William Shakespeare described Lady Macbeth as "the most perfect hostess." Early in the play she describes information she received from the witches as "the perfectest report." Most of us don't have the stature of a James Madison or a William Shakespeare, so it's best to stay away from such usage in everyday business activities.

Here are just a few more examples of misused and overused sentences and phrases heard in the workplace that might be worth avoiding. I've added possible alternatives.

It is what it is." This is usually said in frustration or resignation. It's throwing up one's hands in defeat. We hear this from both staff and managers. From a manager's perspective, however, it could be expressed differently as: "There are other options." Such a sentence indicates the possibility and the probability of improvement.

"No problem." This is often heard after someone says, "Thank you for your help." A better response could be, and should be, simply and politely, "You're welcome."

A chance departure in a workplace often concludes with: "Have a good one." One what? A more appropriate response would be, "Have a good day, a good morning, a good afternoon, or a good evening."

"To tell the truth" or "truthfully" are foolish ways to start a comment because they hint that perhaps some previous comments were not truthful. Simply don't use the comment.

"Look" at the beginning of a sentence comes across as condescending, pompous, and boastful. A better opening is to just start talking.

"You guys" is a frequently used salutation as in "How are you guys this evening?" or "What would you guys like to order?" or "Are you guys being helped?" It is intended to be friendly and informal, but it comes across as presumptuous. Forget the "guys" word. Simply say, "What would you like to order?" or "How are you this evening?" or "Are you being helped?" It sounds much more professional and businesslike.

Because our language is constantly evolving, remember to avoid being caught up in verbal "fads de jour." Stability and consistency are important traits welcomed by both colleagues and customers. And they contribute to developing sound business relationships.

Oh, The Words We Select!

As the pressures of political seasons increase, we hear substantial rhetoric from many directions. I thought about some of the common words in presenter's speeches, and I noticed how certain words show up in everyday use, too.

Without actually counting, one of the most frequently used words is: "Fight." Everyone is promising to "fight" for something. Sounds strong and tough, but I'll bet most of them haven't had a real fight since a lunchbox dispute during recess in the first grade. I have no idea if that's true, of course, but I hope the exaggeration makes a point.

They won't fight, they'll "work," but that doesn't sound very powerful. "Fight" is a word intended to deceive in political speeches, but we must be aware of deception in business dealings, too. We're not elected to serve multiple-year terms.

We can lose our "business terms" overnight.

"Fees" is another deceptive word that shows up in many segments of our daily lives. Don't be fooled. Here are some examples. Airlines now charge baggage "fees," a "fee" for a better seat, and a "fee" for rescheduling a reservation. They don't increase prices because that wouldn't look good. "Fees," however, can be added and manipulated at will.

Even closer to home than air travel are the "fees" parents must pay to provide items and services that should be provided by public school budgets. Because school boards and administrations operate beyond what is provided by taxes, they add "fees" for all kinds of things, including lab fees, book fees, art fees, supply fees, athletic fees, and extra-curricular fees, to name only a few. Such "fees" are simply tax increases without benefit of discussion or the chance to vote.

Here's another interesting word: "Irregardless." It's interesting because it isn't a real word. It sounds "intelligent," though, and is often used by the same people who say "between you and I..." It sounds smart to them, but don't use it!

With increasing frequency, the word, "Look" is used to build a verbal platform before making a statement. It's nothing more than a jumpstart. Often within the sentence that follows "look" we'll hear yet another word: "Fundamental." It seems our language is now filled with "fundamental changes," "fundamental principles," and "fundamental issues."

Once again it's a matter of image over accuracy, and

it becomes redundant and annoying very quickly. Many other words are misused either because of carelessness or because we never learned the right ones. Here is a brief sample of words that are singular or plural. As a reminder, the first word in each pair is the singular one. Medium, media; criterion, criteria; memorandum, memoranda; datum, data. Pay attention, and every day you'll hear many of the plural words used when the singular would be correct.

Our language has thousands of words, and no two words mean exactly the same thing. We use only a few of them, but be careful of your choices. Our words speak volumes about us either in speech or in print. People judge us by the words we use, and even though we might feel that's unfair, it's in our best interest to select the words with care.

In summary, here's a parting thought. *Look, it's up to you and I to literally fight hard to preserve our fundamental language conventions so they remain clear and precise, irregardless of changing social pressures.*

Okay?

Make Your Point With an Economy of Words.

I've written about the need for all of us to be Clear, Complete, and Concise in business communication. I first heard that combination of words when I was in the military. They were – and I assume still are – the mantra for anyone responsible for transmitting information. And, for us in business situations, that mantra is essential to maintain credibility.

If customers can't easily understand what we're saying, they won't try to figure it out. They'll go elsewhere to someone who will be straightforward. When customers are confronted by someone who talks in circles, changes direction in mid-course, and "retracts" or "clarifies" messages, they wonder why they didn't hear straight talk from the start.

Here's a simple thought. "Yes" means yes, and "No" means no. When qualifications are added to those words, customers become suspicious. And they have a right to wonder.

If we don't say clearly what we mean, how can we expect others to have confidence in us as businesspeople or as private individuals?

Recently I thought about that need for clarity, and its absence, in much of what we read and hear today.

On July fourth, I was struck by the clarity and brevity of the documents our Founding Fathers gave us. What they intended to do and why they were going to do it was extremely clear in what they wrote in the Declaration of Independence.

(As a sidebar – if you haven't read the document in a while, take the time to do it. It's a marvelous piece of work.)

I had a teacher in elementary school, Sister Mary Rosita, who told us "Say what you mean, and mean what you say."

This is great advice for elementary school students and for anyone in business today. That describes what our Founders did, and they did it with an exceptional economy of words.

They stated their position using only 1,322 words. Talk about Clear, Complete, and Concise!

Just think of the commitment of those writers and the power of their few words. They stood up to one of the most powerful nations on Earth and said, "No." They said it with no If's, And's, or But's.

Everyone understood what they meant. They maintained that verbal focus and economy when, a decade later, they wrote the U.S. Constitution using only 4,543 words. And everyone understood the new government.

For comparative purposes, the current U.S. Tax Code contains 3.8 million words. That's 870 times the length of the Constitution, and 2,950 times the length of the Declaration of Independence.

Can anyone understand the U.S. Tax Code?

This speaks to the axiom, "Less is more."

We can all learn from reflecting on the value of clarity and the economy of words in our daily activities and experiences.

We're confronted with verbal confusion every day as we review contracts, warranties, guarantees, etc. We'll probably admit that many of these business instruments are constructed and worded in ways that confuse the average person.

Contracts that once said, "You do this, and I'll do that," now require multiple pages of small type to cover any possible real or imagined future conditions. In many respects, such documents devote more time and attention to the "If" and "Might" than to the "Do."

As information moves down from layer to layer in business organizations, more restrictions and conditions are added. When everyone has had a chance to add his "own two cents," we end up with a big pile of change which we may or may not understand and which may or may not even reflect what the original writer intended. What's the value of that?

Sister Mary Rosita was right, and our Founding Fathers presented us with a sterling model for being clear, complete, and concise. Let's all hope we learn from those lessons.

Just Between You and I

We're judged by the words we use, so let's look at a couple of areas which are problems but are easily corrected.

The first focuses on being careful how we spell words in print. This has become increasingly important as more of us do our own typing and then rely on computers to check our spelling. Spell checking software will tell us if a word is spelled correctly, but it won't tell us if we have used the right word. That's our responsibility. The second suggests we use our ears to select the correct words. When talking, it helps if we listen carefully to what we're saying.

Let's begin with correct spelling and look at one of the most common errors: confusing *your* and *you're*. Our grammar teachers taught us *your* is a possessive, and *you're* is a contraction for *you are*. That's pretty simple, but we see it misused every day. I'm not sure if the cause is carelessness or ignorance. What I am sure of, however, is many of our readers know the difference, and they make judgments about our intelligence and our ability. It's simple. If you mean, *you are*, use *you're.* Nothing complicated or difficult about that! If you mean someone owns something, use *your.* Again, simple. The first word in that last paragraph is another example of misuse. *It's* is a contraction for "It is," but *Its* shows possession. Once again, simple.

We know what we intend to communicate but, all too often, we don't deliver it correctly. In a previous section, I described advice my first grade teacher gave to her students. "Say what you mean, and mean what you say." That same advice transfers to, "Write what you mean, and mean what you write."

Here's another one that is often misused. You decide

if it's carelessness or ignorance. With this one, we have three options: *they're, their,* and *there.* The distinction is easy. *They're* is a contraction for "they are;" *their* is a possessive, and an heir inherits; and *there*, like *here*, is a place.

Many other pairs and triads sound alike and have a strange sounding name: homonym – words that sound alike but have very different meanings. They include: site, cite, sight; capital, capitol; wait, weight; council, counsel; and a host of others we can't cover here. If you're not sure of the meanings just check a dictionary in print or on line. Remind yourself of the differences in order to avoid future errors. A little thought and care will remove the errors, so why make an issue of this? That's simple and worth repeating. In business, people judge us by the words we use. The impression we make on customers and colleagues is influenced by what we say and how we say it.

This second section relates specifically to spoken communication – what listeners hear. No spelling necessary here. (There's another homonym.)

These errors are interesting because, although most people know what is correct, many select the wrong words in order to sound "intellectual." Perhaps the most frequent error is in misusing "I" and "me." Even without grammar rules, we can usually tell what's correct and incorrect just by how it sounds to us. We hear people saying things like, "If it's up to Charles and I, we would..." The easiest way to check this is to eliminate Charles, and listen to how it sounds if you say, "If it's up to I..." You know that's wrong just by how strange it sounds. Obviously it should be "Charles and me."

Here's another common one heard frequently, even from professional broadcasters who should know better. "*Just between you and I*, it's important that we consider..." "Between you and I" is *Always Wrong*! Don't say it! For anyone who might think it sounds "intellectual," "sophisticated," or "impressive," be warned. It doesn't!

These two areas of effective communication are good reminders of the need to select options deliberately in order to project the professional impression we want in business.

Who Says So?

It's easy to intimidate or impress people. Just put on the cloak of an institution, and let it do the talking for you. For example, when a letter containing bad news arrives in a mailbox, many people feel pressured to do something they didn't intend to do when they see the return address. However, taking a brief pause and considering the source of the information can make a big difference. Just look at these two sentences:

"The insurance company cancelled my policy."

"Charlie Jones cancelled my policy."

Which one is more likely to induce a panic response? The first one, of course, because it came from an institution. But remember this. No institution ever wrote a letter! Only a person can write a letter!

Here are a couple of examples demonstrating the power of the "anonymous author," and they raise the specter of having to "fight City Hall." An acquaintance of mine told me how a letter from the Environmental Protection Agency (EPA) informed him he cannot expand his dock because of some new sea grass growing in the area. A neighbor wants to build a patio in his back yard, but the zoning board wrote, informing him it won't issue a permit.

Life becomes more manageable and less frightening, however, when we realize a missive was prepared by some person sitting at a desk somewhere, not by an institution or by an agency. Since this "panic" response happens frequently, here's a suggestion that can help reduce anxiety. Find out who wrote the letter. Get a name and a phone number. Place a call and talk to him or her. The Internet has made it easier to accomplish that task today than it was a decade ago. It's impossible to talk to an institution, but it's easy to talk to a person. This is an important mindset, and it applies in many areas.

When I entered military service, a friend who served many years as a military officer gave me an interesting piece of advice. Initially, I didn't believe him because it was contrary to everything I thought I knew about the military.

He told me, "During your service time, you'll be subjected to many official orders. Some you'll like, some you won't. Of course, you must obey legitimate orders, but always remember, some enlisted clerk somewhere typed those orders. If you want to do something other than what the orders direct, find some other enlisted clerk who can legally type other orders."

When I was eventually in a situation in which it was appropriate to try out his advice, I did. It worked. He was right.

Here's another tactic that causes readers to react unnecessarily. Many institutional directives are written in passive voice, and read like this:

"Your policy has been cancelled."

"Your permit has been denied."

That wording alone is intimidating because it seems to be final and absolute rather than a "work in progress." Well-placed questions about such sentences can often reverse a decision or modify directed action. If and when you receive such a communication: first find out who wrote it, ask specifically who made the decision, ask why. You are entitled to an explanation. Worst-case scenario, you'll simply understand better the reasons behind the negative decision. Best-case scenario, you'll get that person to change the decision. That's well worth the effort!

"But wait – there's more!"

As the legendary radio personality, Paul Harvey often said, "Here's the rest of the story." When you are the one writing those letters, use these same tactics to your advantage. Write in passive voice. Don't take personal responsibility for decisions or conclusions. Let the reader believe the directions are coming from a powerful impersonal source. The tactic will give you a distinct advantage. By knowing how the system works, you'll be able to use it when you're sending a message, and you'll be aware of it when you're receiving one.

When all the players know the rules of any contest, the competition is always more interesting.

CHAPTER 5

Writing Tips

The words we put on paper or on screens speak volumes about us, and they can last forever. Do what is necessary to demonstrate knowledge of your material and your tools. Lead by example. Use every communication tool correctly, and others will be more inclined to follow your lead. Teach by example.

Most of us learned how to write while we were in school. Some of us learned to write well, but others saw writing as a chore to be avoided at all costs. When we had to write "compositions," we put it off until the last possible moment and, sometimes, we swore our "dog ate the paper." No teacher ever believed that excuse, but it seemed to have many lives over the years.

There are a couple of major differences between school writing and business writing. They include the simple fact that in school we were rewarded for writing long papers. In business, however, brevity and clarity are more important than bulk.

This section examines a variety of writing techniques and offers examples of how to make writing effective. The specific techniques covered can go a long way to ease the strains of writing and demonstrate how writing on paper or online can be Clear, Complete, and Concise.

Too Many Words, Too Little Impact

Voltaire said, "The secret of being a bore is to tell everything." Many of us do precisely that. We give too much information because we confuse quantity with quality. Here's an example, but you can apply the concept to many aspects of your business.

Recently I reviewed a number of corporate mission statements and I realized, although the corporate names varied, for the most part, all the mission statements were the same. Every company described itself as "the best," "the strongest," "the most reliable," and "the industry leader." It promised to deliver "high quality," "reliable products," "excellent customer service," at "fair prices," while using "the latest technology," "modern methods," and "best practices."

Sound familiar?

A good mission statement describes the drive and the direction of a company. It also drives employee behavior and assures customer understanding. A clear mission statement is like military marching orders describing what will be done to accomplish a task. It provides needed direction, guidance, and motivation because sooner or later everyone has to deliver what is promised.

When everyone in a company understands what the mission statement is and what it means, every worker becomes that statement and behaves in ways that demonstrate the mission. What a work force does on a regular basis communicates strong messages about a company to everyone who comes in contact with it. But mission statements are often too long. The people who write them choose their words carefully, and the words read well. They also look good in a framed plaque, but most people can't say them. The true message gets lost because the statement is so wordy and convoluted.

What can we do to fix this? Try this, and see what happens.

Read your corporate mission statement, or other appropriate document, and count the words. Now ask yourself, "What does this mean?" Answer that question out loud, and write your response exactly as you said it. Count those words. You probably used half as many words as in the original. Repeat the steps, and the word count will likely be cut in half again. Obviously, it won't be precisely half, but there will be a significant reduction.

This writing discipline is a kind of "minimal speech" where you get to the heart of the matter almost immediately. This economy of words can be applied to many aspects of a company and the manner in which we communicate to our customers.

Because of habits, education, and social conventions, the sentences we speak are usually about half as long as the sentences we write. Use that spoken brevity to focus your mission statement. Use it with all customer communications. Remember this simple guideline. If you can't say it, you may not do it because you don't fully understand it.

Here are a few questions for practice. See if you can answer them in six or fewer words and still provide adequate information. Not everything – just enough. I'm not suggesting you construct a "Dick and Jane" reading primer here. I'm suggesting brevity, clarity, and precision.

Try these questions for starters. What does your company (or department or division) do? What do you want your customers to know about your company? What do you (as an individual) do? How do you do it?

When you specify and focus these answers within a handful of words, everyone in your company will be able to remember and to deliver the information. When messages are clear and easy to say, clear and deliberate actions follow. The messages we construct and deliver to our customers will then be: *Clear* to them. The message is for them, not for us. We already know it. *Concise.* Keep it short and easy to follow. *Complete* Not everything you know, only what your customers need.

Voltaire was right. Telling our customers everything we know about our company can bore them. It can also confuse and frustrate them.

Obviously, that's never good for business.

Give Your E-Mails a Fighting Chance with a Grabber.

Did you ever wonder why anyone reads one specific e-mail but skips another? Consider this. Every e-mail ends up on a computer screen sandwiched in with lots of other e-mails, and each one of them is competing for a reader's attention. Sometimes the number of e-mails on that screen can be overpowering and the sheer number can cause our eyes to glaze over. Many of them may be just plain junk or spam, but, nevertheless, readers still have to deal with them and decide what to read right away, what to delay, and what to delete.

What can we do to increase the probability they will read our e-mails? Although the name of the sender is often a major decision factor, usually the *subject line* is what gets a reader's attention, or persuades him to keep looking for something more interesting and valuable. The subject line should be the "grabber," so construct it carefully and deliberately. Because it's the first thing the reader sees, make it work for you. Don't just write the first thing that comes to mind. And don't risk being careless. In many respects, the subject line is advertising the message. It's a way to entice a reader to follow our lead. We're competing with all the other e-mails on the screen so we need to find ways to stand out from the crowd.

A good subject line should accomplish two tasks. *First*, it should create interest. *Second*, it should preview the content of the message. It's a headline, and it should encourage the reader to read what we wrote.

Here are a couple of examples of what we can do to entice a reader by manipulating just a few words. Use "special" words to add substance and interest to the subject line. Look at the difference a few well-chosen words can make in creating that initial impression in these examples:

Cost Projections vs. *Alarming* Cost Projections

Price Increase vs. *Surprising* Price Increase

Seasonal Shifts vs. *Unexpected* Seasonal Shifts

Headquarters Relocation vs. Headquarters Relocation *to Tallahassee*.

You see? By adding a word or two, the subject line becomes much more than a placeholder on the computer screen. Suddenly, it's an invitation, an enticement, or a warning. A well-constructed subject line can turn a simple message into a "must read" for the receiver.

Here's a little exercise to try when you have a few minutes. Pull up some of the e-mails you sent during the past couple of weeks and look at each subject line. Ask yourself, "Did this really grab the reader?"

Then ask yourself how you could have made it more compelling by adding a special word or two. What words did you select? What happened to the impact of the subject line?

Now, here's something else to consider. Don't write the subject line as soon as you type in the reader's address. Wait a while. Write the entire message first, then ask, "What does this really say, and what can I add to encourage the receiver to read it?"

As with a newspaper or a book, the content is completed first, and then the headline or title is written. Both the headline and the title are the "grabbers," and they work!

Do the same thing for e-mails. All the messages we send have a great deal of competition for the reader's time and attention so get a competitive advantage with an enticing "grabber."

It might take a few extra moments to come up with the right words, but that extra time will be worth it if the message is read.

Entice and encourage readers to read the message. Don't simply hope and assume they'll read it. That's too risky.

Effective business communication isn't about taking risks. It's about being clear and effective. We wrote that e-mail message in the first place because we had something important to say.

Use this subject line focus technique, and be sure it will be read.

"Do-It-Yourself" Business Communication

In a galaxy far away and long ago, there existed items like dictating machines, typing pools, secretaries, and stenographers. Now, they're all gone. Evolution has made them obsolete, and sophisticated technologies like the computer have replaced all but a few remaining hardy species.

We usually see these developments as good because data and information now move much faster and through more channels than ever before. But that progress has resulted in an interesting shift of responsibilities. In those bygone days, for example, business executives did what they did well. They talked. They dictated letters and other material into a recording device or directly to a live person. Others then did what they did well. They typed the letters using correct formats, grammar, spelling, syntax, etc. That division of labor produced good material quickly and accurately.

Now all of that has changed. Today, just about everyone in business is a typist, and many of us aren't very good at it. We certainly don't do it as well as the long-ago specialists did. Like many of my contemporaries, I never learned the correct way to type. I didn't have to because there was always someone there to do that. But now, the computer has enabled – perhaps forced – all of us to be do-it-yourself typists. I'm doing okay, and I'm making progress. I'm no longer a one-finger typist. In fact, I'm up to about five fingers on a regular basis, but I still rely heavily on the delete key and spell checking software.

This shift of responsibility, however, requires all of us to be more careful and aware of the messages we send via e-mail and snail mail. In most instances we are now our own editors, and no one "fixes" our mistakes or revises our material to make it look good before it is sent.

Now here is the dilemma. While everyone in the business community is doing more and more writing, schools are requiring students to do less and less writing. Some schools are even allowing students to "text" answers to test questions. If students don't learn to write well while in school, when will they learn the skill? Will their future employers have to provide remedial writing classes? Who will be responsible to teach them? Or will employers simply allow the poor writing to continue? Of course not, but something has to change.

Statistics from the U.S. Department of Education show that 30% of college freshmen are enrolled in remedial classes. In the California State University system, 46% of the students were enrolled in remedial English classes. Children aren't learning to write in grammar school or in high school. Hopefully, they'll learn in college, but what a waste of time that is. College shouldn't be the place where students try to master what should have been learned years earlier.

It would be easy for us in the business community to judge the schools and say the current situation is terrible. More importantly, though, we should find ways to assist our academic colleagues by stressing the importance of good communication skills every time we are in contact with young people. There are plenty of opportunities for us to do it. We speak at back-to-school sessions, we interview job candidates, we talk to our children and their friends, we advertise our products and services in a variety of venues used by young people. We should use our influence and contacts to encourage teachers, administrators, and citizens to ensure that students are provided with every possible opportunity to master this important skill. But in addition to those opportunities, we have to communicate the importance of these skills directly to the students.

If the business community conveys the belief that being able to write well is an essential skill, and teachers require high quality performance from their students, we'll all be able to continue to move forward in concert with the continuing technological changes.

If we expect the people we hire in the years ahead to continue being "do-it-yourself" writers, we'd better be sure all of them have the right tools and know how to use them.

What Does Your E-mail Say?

For most of us e-mail is a regular part of our day. We check the incoming mail frequently regardless if we are at the office, at home, or on the road. And we send out messages, sometimes short bursts of data, and other times long, detailed compositions. Electronic mail, however, poses a couple of problems. First, it often doesn't look very good, because the mass of material on the screen requires the reader to plow through it. Second, it isn't written very well. Even when the reader works hard to plow through the data, the point of the e-mail is often lost.

We've all received that kind of electronic junk mail, and we know how we react to it. Years ago, a character in a comic strip said, "We have met the enemy, and they is us." In order to avoid being the "enemy" and writing electronic junk mail here are a few tips. Write a Subject Line that is a "grabber." Every piece of e-mail competes with every other piece of e-mail for the reader's attention. Make your subject line an interesting headline that contributes two elements. It attracts attention and gives a preview of what will be covered. Look at the difference between these two examples: "New Headquarters Location" vs. "Plans to move Headquarters to Miami Beach." One is a grabber, the other isn't. Which would you read?

Now, here's another suggestion. Write the subject line after you compose the e-mail. Like a newspaper headline or a book title, the subject line should be the final step in the production process. Next, get to your point quickly. Put the message, the reason you are sending the e-mail in the first paragraph. If you're sending a very short e-mail, put the message in the first sentence. Don't make a reader work hard to find out what you're thinking.

Keep the language simple. We've all seen sentences that say something like this, "It would be appropriate for the parties to convene and discuss possibilities to evaluate subsequent actions." That sentence means, "Let's meet to decide what to do next." So say it that way. Use the same language in your e-mail you would use face-to-face.

Use appropriate software to check spelling, but don't rely on it. Software will tell you if a word is spelled correctly, but it won't tell you if it is the correct word. That's up to you. Spelling software can't tell the difference between "your," "yore," and you're," but the readers can.

Make the e-mail look good. Use both upper and lower case letters just as you do when writing on paper. Indent. Double space. Punctuate correctly. Many of us try to fool ourselves into being too casual by thinking, "It's only e-mail." That seems to give us permission to be careless. But, when you reader hits the "Print" button on the computer that e-mail is now hard copy, and it lives forever.

Be careful about forwarding messages you receive. Adding "FYI" to those messages adds bulk but not necessarily content to your reader's day. By all means, send on information if it will be of value to your reader, but don't forward something if it isn't necessary.

Leave plenty of space around your words. Openness is inviting. When your text looks good, it will be read. How many times have you decided not to read an e-mail because it looked too cumbersome to get through quickly? If you leave such e-mails for later, so will your reader.

Follow these tips and your e-mails will show you respect your readers and their time. You'll demonstrate you used your time and effort to write a message that was clear, concise, and easy to understand. Research has demonstrated that the quality of writing has declined as the use of e-mail has increased. Such writing demonstrates a lack of interest and respect for the people who receive those messages. What we write and how we write it creates an impression on our readers, and that impression is often as important in business as the content is.

Here's a final thought. Just because e-mail transmits information quickly doesn't mean it has to be written quickly.

Clear Definitions Are Essential.

Because you are directly involved in the daily activities of your company, or division, or department you know more about it than anyone else. That's often good news and bad news when you're asked simple questions.

Here's a little test. Write an answer to this question. "What does your company (or division or department) do?" Stop reading for a moment. Write the answer and then continue reading. Now count the number of words

146 J. Robert Parkinson, Ph.D.

you used to answer the question. Make believe you really don't know much about your company. Does this written answer give you sufficient and clear information? Does it accurately describe your company? Do you understand the description? If so, well done. If not, why not?

Now write the description again, but use about half the number of words you used the first time. Reread your new version, and determine if it would be a clear explanation to someone coming upon the description for the first time. Once more, write an even shorter description. Which version would most likely "grab" a reader or a listener? Which one invites interest and a follow up? In most instances, when I've used this technique in seminars, the consensus is the same. The short one is the most difficult to write, but it is the one most likely to "grab" a reader or a listening audience.

So here's another question. If most people think the short version is best, why do so many people in companies and organizations write the long versions? Is it because they don't want to spend the time and effort needed to produce the short one? Is it because they don't know how to write a good short one? Or is it because they just don't care?

That third question is probably an unlikely response. The second one is a possibility, and it can easily be corrected with some instruction. The first one seems most probable, and it deserves immediate attention because it might demonstrate an attitude that can lead to even greater communication problems and corporate difficulties.

The problem is this: If companies, or more accurately the people who represent companies, don't use their time well to produce their best and clearest messages, the receivers of those messages have to do all the hard work. They have to use their time and their energy to "figure out" what the writer or speaker intended to convey. That doesn't make sense. The reader shouldn't have to work, and in most cases won't work to understand unclear messages. They'll look elsewhere which might lead them to your competition. No business and no corporate representatives want to do that.

So here's a suggestion and a challenge. Take a little time and write answers to the following questions just as you did to that first one. Writing the answers, by the way, is more valuable than just thinking about them because of the discipline of the blank piece of paper!

If we simply think about how to say or do something, we often fool ourselves into believing we really can communicate and articulate the information clearly and accurately. The act of writing, however, makes it necessary to actually construct the thoughts on paper. If you can't write a thought on a piece of paper or on a computer screen, you probably won't communicate it clearly when you try to say it.

Now, here are those other questions to add to the What does your company do? How does it do that? What can you do for your customers and clients? How will you do that?

When we were all in school, we learned that the more we wrote on an examination or in a term paper the better the grade we would receive. And most of us used that knowledge and skill to our advantage. But we're not in school any more. The rules in the business world are different, and the expectations of our clients are different than in our earlier school days. It's in our own best interest to recognize that a different style is appropriate in business writing. Deliver short, clear, and direct information in a way that every reader and listener will understand immediately.

Remember how the work of architect Ludwig Mies van der Rohe was described? "Less is more." Apply that principle to your business messages. The less verbiage you put in front of your reader and listener the more they'll understand what you mean.

It's worth a try – and a little time.

Looooooong Letters

Does anyone read the long four-page letters that arrive in personal mailboxes? You know, the letters that are filled with the "latest," "greatest," and "most dangerous." All those words are intended to evoke an immediate reaction and fast response! Many of the sentences are underlined and emphasized with bold-faced type to prompt immediate action. Also, four-pages seem to be the accepted template for these "important" documents.

In a single week, I've received seven of them! Again, I ask, "Does anyone read them? Do they inform, inspire, intrigue, or are they simply thrown into the trash?" It's interesting to note the recent increased frequency of these letters – especially from politicians, political organizations, and special-interest groups. Their sense of urgency is almost overpowering – or comical. But do people read four-page letters? Most people today are either too busy or too impatient to spend their time reading such unsolicited material. With the increasing use of text messages, that impatience will continue to increase. So why produce such verbose letters?

Readers want information quickly, and they want it in an easy to process format. A previous section included this suggestion: "In order to be a good writer, think like your reader."

It's rather naive for a writer to think anyone would take the time to read an unsolicited four-page letter. Remember the general directive about writing these days is "keep it simple." Many of the letters that show up in mailboxes make a point, then make it again, and make it again, then again with a strong plea to send money to assure the point will be made yet again.

If you are ever responsible for writing such material, here's something to consider. Your content should be of interest and value to your reader, not a vehicle to demonstrate how much you know.

Here's a productive sequence: Make your point. Back it up. Stop. Keep everything simple and short. Begin by telling your reader what you want. Be specific. Make your point early. Next, tell the reader why it's important for him or for her to do what you're recommending. The supporting material converts your point from being an opinion to being a sound defensible position.

Finally, describe the next steps the reader should take. Keep the vocabulary simple, the sentences short, and the language clear. If you fill two pages, you've probably included too much. Remember that old bit of advice about excessive information. When someone asks you what time it is, tell him. Don't teach him how to build a wristwatch.

Remember, don't attempt to include everything you know. Select the content based upon what your audience needs. Now write your first draft. Before you commit that draft to its final form ask yourself this question. "What can I leave out, and still make my point?" Then leave out whatever is unnecessary or redundant. You now have something that will likely be read, understood, and get the results you want.

If I'm right about most people not reading the four-page letters, wouldn't it make sense to stop writing them? Writing and distributing such material represents a significant cost for any organization because someone has to gather the data, and then someone else has to write the letter. Another someone then edits and approves the material. Then it has to be printed, and a mailing list has to be prepared. An entire package of material is then assembled, because there is usually material in addition to the four-page letter.

The package is put into the mail, the US Postal Service takes over, and ultimately the envelopes arrive in mailboxes. That's the point at which most of the letters are thrown into the trash. What a system!

Follow the suggested three-step sequence, and the result will more likely be read because the finished product will be considerably shorter than four pages,

That's a good thing because the environmentalists tell us you'll probably save some trees.

That might make you feel good, too.

CHAPTER 6

Customer Service

Actions speak louder than words. Show, don't just tell. Lead by example.

We've all heard these precepts in the past, but all too often we forget to demonstrate them. Such demonstrations will pull others to action. Just telling others how to behave doesn't work.

Without customers there is no business. There might be ideas and inventory and buildings, but that's not business. Business requires someone providing a service or product that someone else purchases. But there's much more than selling and buying. To continue doing business over time, customers must continue to visit the office or the store. The only way to assure that happens is to take good care of the customer each time he or she enters the establishment.

Some businesspeople seem to know instinctively what to do to keep their customers, but many don't. They are too concerned with their own needs, interests, and desires rather than those of the customer. It's hard to fathom, but some businesspeople treat customers as if they are intruding on their time or facilities. To them, customers are a bother. They behave in ways that convey those messages to their customers.

That's just plain stupid!

Here are tales of good customer service, and bad customer service. Some of the bad examples are hard to believe, but they all happened.

Pick Two.

Recently I was in a store at a resort area and saw a sign that read, "Quality, Price, Service (Pick Two)." Obviously it was intended to be a joke, but as I thought about it, that choice is often required in many business establishments. Of course, the choice is never voiced to customers by management, but employees (Associates) often force the issue.

Employees usually can't do anything about the first two options – Quality and Price– but they are "in charge" of the Service. For the continued success of any business, the service is what retains or replaces customers. The Quality and Price of offerings are usually similar from establishment to establishment; it's the Service that makes the impression. Most products are available in a variety of competing locations, so customers have choices. How they are treated in those various places makes a customer loyal or lost.

An old adage in communication – and in business – states: "Audiences (customers) won't remember exactly what you said. They won't remember precisely what you did. But they will never forget how you made them feel."

To retain customers, it's important to make them feel welcome – not that they are being a bother or making outlandish requests. Employees should be "nice" to customers. This isn't Pollyanna, it's just good business. And, it's easy! It's also just as easy for an employee to be an annoying jerk.

Here are two examples – both from retail establishments. When paying for a $48 order, a man handed a $100 bill to a cashier saying, "I'm sorry, but aside from 2 singles, this is the only bill I have."

The cashier pursed her lips, took the bill, held it up to the light, slapped it on the counter, drew a line across the bill to check its authenticity with the magic pen used in stores, and made the change. She never said a word to him, but she made him feel as if he had done something wrong.

A similar event occurred in a restaurant when a patron attempted to pay for his take-out sandwich with a $50 bill. With "attitude" the clerk said, "I don't know if we can change that." The patron replied, "Then I guess I'll get my sandwich for free."

Without comment, the clerk opened the cash drawer and found ample currency to make the change. Leaving the sandwich and a bag of chips on the counter, he started to walk away when the patron said, "May I have a bag, please?" Again, without a word, the clerk put the items in a bag and continued walking away. From the expression on the patron's face, my guess is he'll find a different sandwich shop the next time he's hungry. The clerk didn't care. That's just one more customer he won't have to wait on, but management would care if they learned about the clerk's behavior.

In the quest for "equal opportunity," and not to pick on only food service operations, here's one from a local government agency office. After waiting in a long line, a woman's turn came. The clerk, however, made a phone call, turned her back to everyone in line, hung up the phone, stood up, and walked away. Without a word. When she returned, she sat down and, while still looking at her countertop, called out, "Next."

The overall impression was that the woman was interrupting the clerk's day, and the clerk communicated that message.

The disconnect was clear. The clerk was there to provide a designated and reasonable service for which the woman had waited, but she was made to feel she was intruding on the clerk's time or priorities.

There are many more examples, but these should suffice to make the point.

The fix is easy. Take the time to look people in the eye when talking to them, and always use a positive, pleasant, and reassuring tone of voice. That's all there is to it!

Customers will remember how they felt about doing business with you.

Behaviors Have Consequences.

Whatever we do during the course of our business – and personal – days, produces reactions from our customers, colleagues, and social acquaintances.

Many of the behaviors are unintended, and daily pressures sometimes cause them, so here's an idea that might help avoid inappropriate reactions.

Attitude is a powerful factor that influences our behavior and how we view situations and conditions.

Consider this definition of attitude my co-author and I used in our book, *Becoming a Successful Manager*, "An attitude is a state of mind and a predisposition to action based on what you tell yourself.

"Attitudes precede actions; positive attitudes lead to productive actions; negative attitudes lead to unproductive actions."

From the book, here's an example showing how attitudes work, and how what we call "self-talk," can provide control and direction.

The customer-service department of a Midwest company was receiving frequent complaints. Specifically, people said customer service representatives treated them rudely. They were left on hold for what seemed to be forever, disconnected while waiting to be helped, and then not given the help they hoped to receive. These complaints had gone on for almost a year and were accompanied by a steady decline in sales. During a meeting we had with the five-person department, we asked, "When the phone rings, what do you tell yourself before you answer it?"

We received blank stares and no immediate responses. With some encouragement, though, everyone eventually related a variation of the same negative self-talk comment: "Here comes another complainer!"

After discussing the effect self-talk can have on behavior, we suggested they tell themselves something else when the phone rings. For instance: "This caller has a problem. My job is to help him or her to solve that problem, and I can do that. I'm a valuable resource to this person in trouble." As part of the solution, they also adopted the greeting, "How can I help you?" when answering the phone.

This simple question was more than words. It was a genuine positive attitude, revealed in their tone of voice that said, "I want to help you."

Within a month, the vice president of operations

started receiving feedback praising the customer service department.

The lesson learned was this: If your attitude is negative, it will come through, but if your attitude is positive, that, too, will come through.

This positive attitude suggestion isn't a "magic bullet" that will solve all your problems immediately, but it will go a long way toward influencing and reshaping behavior. It's a kind of self-fulfilling prophecy.

We've all done this to ourselves without even thinking about it.

There may have been a time you were invited to go to a meeting you didn't want to attend but didn't have an option.

If you chose a negative attitude and told yourself the meeting would be a waste of time, it was. On the other hand, if you had chosen a positive attitude and told yourself, "This is a tight time, but as long as I have to go, I'll see if I can learn something I might have missed out on had I not attended," you did.

In all likelihood whichever attitude you choose will result in your prediction coming true. When we have a strong belief about the outcome of a relationship or an impending experience, we do everything in our power to make that belief come true.

It's a pretty safe bet to say that attitudes are responsible for creating and perpetuating our successes and failures as well as the quality of our relationships.

Business is all about building and maintaining relationships, and directing attitudes by this self-talk can be a great help for all of us.

I've written this line before: People might forget exactly what you say, and they might forget precisely what you do, but they will never forget how you make them feel.

Use this "self-talk" technique. See how your attitude can shape your behavior.

Customer Service Made Easy

It's interesting how some people in businesses say and do things that are comfortable and convenient for them without giving any thought to how their customers might react.

Just a few weeks ago, my wife and I had an encounter with a Customer Relations representative of a major hotel chain. We were exploring a time-share possibility, but we were summarily "dismissed" and directed to the exit because we didn't agree to make an immediate, on-the-spot purchase. No, "Thank you for coming." Not even a handshake. Only an arm wave directing us to the door. Clearly, we were no longer wanted, and we were in the way.

Like that sales staff, some business people behave in ways that may make them "feel good" but not necessarily in ways that will help them "be good." Being good in this context refers to demonstrating concern and appreciation for, as well as providing assistance to customers. For customers, some business places can be confusing, even intimidating.

For people working in those places, however, the environment and the activities are familiar.

Regardless of the business we're in, everything is – or should be – about our customers and about customer service. Tom Peters, the customer service guru, summed up all that needs to be done in one sentence. He said, "Find out what the customer wants, and give it to him." A short list of customer "wants" includes: product or service knowledge, of course, assistance, attention, courtesy, information, and direction. But there is something else a customer expects and deserves – Respect. We certainly didn't get that!

Here are some of the behaviors we can use to provide that deserved respect. They're simple, but they're powerful. Greet the customer. Acknowledge the customer's presence with a smile, a nod, maybe a "Hello" or "How are you?" But don't pounce, and don't shadow the customer. Give him or her plenty of space, and be ready and available to provide assistance when it is requested. When talking with the customer, look him or her in the eye. Don't look at your computer screen, don't flip through the pages of a manual, and never look over his or her shoulder searching for someone else. Look at, and talk to only that person. Show the customer, at that moment, he or she is the most important person in the world. Good eye contact will communicate that message.

Listen attentively to what the customer has to say. If you don't listen well, you might find yourself solving the wrong problem, and that doesn't really solve anything. Use language the customer will understand. Have a conversation. No jargon, technical terminology, or acronyms. Those things might impress your colleagues, but they probably won't help your customer. Speak clearly and slowly. A high-speed answer might be misunderstood, and possibly cast you as impatient. When a customer suspects impatience, it usually leads to annoyance – and to the nearest exit.

Devote all the time necessary to solve the problem. After all, the customer took the time to come to your location, so contribute your time to finding the solution. You might be busy and running late, but that's not the customer's fault. Honor the customer's privacy by not invading his "space." Keep your distance to assure comfort. If appropriate, shake hands, but no other "touching." That handshake should be base of thumb to base of thumb. Firm but not "crushing."

All of these suggestions are obvious, but all too often we overlook them. The behaviors are all "common sense," but a colleague of mine says, "They may be common sense, but they aren't common practice."

He's right.

If we work at it, and make these techniques common practice in all of our contacts, personal and social as well as business, everyone benefits.

That's certainly worth the effort.

That Customer Service Rep lost us and perhaps many other possible purchasers to whom we've told this story. But, she'll never know it.

What Customer Service?

The term "customer service" has become an oxymoron. Businesses exist to provide products and services to customers. Since customers are the reason for any business, it just makes sense to treat them well. The customer may not be "always right," but he's always the customer – the one with the money. Why then do so many companies make it difficult to do business with them? Here are a couple of instances that provoked that question.

Recently I spent an hour and a half with a total of seven "customer service specialists" on the other side of the world. I had a simple request, but I received no simple solution. This is what happened. While traveling on a major US airline I had to change a reservation. The agent at the departure gate told me I would receive a receipt for the additional stand-by fee when I landed. Seemed strange, but I accepted his direction. I didn't get the receipt when I landed so I called "customer service."

All I wanted was to have a receipt sent to me via e-mail since I had already completed the flight. The 800 number connected me with "David" who told me I would have to make the request online. He couldn't help. I asked for a supervisor and was then connected to "Sylvia," then "Dana," then "Helen," and two others whose names I don't remember.

No one helped.

Eventually I was told to go online and check "Refunds" even though that's not what I wanted.

"That's how we issue receipts," number 6 told me. Strange system.

Finally, number 7 checked her computer – as numbers 1 thru 6 could have, and should have, done and saw that no fee had been charged. Therefore no receipt was necessary. I had just wasted an hour and a half. So much for "customer service."

Here's another airline related "customer service" incident. My wife made a hotel reservation through an airline representative when booking a flight. When she didn't receive a confirmation, she called the hotel and was told she had to contact the airline since they had made the reservation. She called the airline and that representative told her she had to call the hotel. "They should take care of it," she was told. Another run around.

With increasing frequency, calls to 800 number customer service locations result in a hand-off rather than assistance.

Baseball fans will recognize this as the old Chicago Cubs "Tinker to Evers to Chance" triple play. Lots of movement by the players, but "You're all out."

Customer service stories are filled with misinformation and multiple-option phone menus that are supposed to "provide better service." In almost every case such menus begin by telling the caller to go online even though the caller already made a decision to place a phone call to talk to a person rather than to type a message into a computer!

We all know such automated systems are cost-effective for a company, but a customer's time is valuable, too.

When the representatives with the fake names answer the phone, companies expect customers to be fooled into thinking they're talking to someone local. Customers aren't stupid, but many companies treat them that way.

Here's a simple suggestion for all businesses. When offering "customer service" in any medium be sure the representatives can indeed provide the service. Don't promise something you can't deliver. When customers get a run-around rather than an answer, the end result is more anger at the situation than at what produced the request in the first place.

True customer service should be a constant reality, not a confusing rarity. In most instances, it's just as easy to do things correctly in the first place as it is to do them poorly.

When companies respect the time and intelligence of customers asking for assistance, those customers will be more likely to respect the time and commitment of the company.

A productive trade-off.

Customers Deserve Respect, Too.

We just discussed the need and value of showing respect to co-workers and colleagues. Now, let's look at the importance of showing respect for customers - and potential customers.

All too often, without intent, we insult some of our customers by talking down to them and by saying to them, "Because you're not very smart, we have to help you and do things for you." Of course, we don't use those exact words, but that's the message we send.

I thought about that recently when I was in a "big box" store and saw this sign on a display of light bulbs. "Six for $6. That's just a dollar each." Now, if a customer couldn't figure that out for himself, he shouldn't be anywhere near an electric socket!

It seems clear whoever drew or directed the making of that sign thought very little of the intelligence of the customer. It's possible though that the sign maker was trying to be funny or cleaver, but it's risky to attempt to be a comedian if you aren't one. And even good professional comedians sometimes insult and offend their audiences by using the wrong words.

Another type of insulting behavior is evident in many television commercials and situation comedies. Two specific examples come to mind. Perhaps you've seen these or can recall others equally offensive. In a series of retail store commercials, two salesmen dress up in outlandish clownish costumes and shout silly dialogue at viewers to come to their store and spend their money on "good deals."

It's remarkable that any sensible adults (the spokespeople) would assume such behavior would persuade other adults to spend many hard earned dollars on their products. That certainly doesn't exhibit a high opinion of the potential customers if they can be fooled and persuaded so easily.

It's easy to find other examples of disrespect of viewers on television. Perhaps you've already noticed the low esteem in which advertisers hold men in commercials. Think of the number of times you've seen "stupid" men. Fathers, for example, are usually portrayed as incompetent, clumsy buffoons who are outsmarted by their precocious children or simply tolerated by their spouses.

Why would an advertiser think that insulting the intelligence of a potential male customer would encourage him to purchase the advertised product or service?

That attitude is truly disrespectful!

Staying with television commercials a little longer, here's something else to consider. Viewers today are used to, and expect to see high quality production in all visual media. That's because the preponderance of their experience has been viewing high quality commercial programs and motion pictures. It takes time, talent, and experience to produce that quality. When a low budget, poor quality, poorly written commercial is delivered in an amateurish fashion, it's expecting a great deal of viewers to watch and listen. Expecting them to pay attention and hoping they will eventually make a purchase insults the intelligence of the viewer.

Now, I'm not accusing any of the producers of these messages of deliberately insulting their audiences. I'm sure that isn't their intention. What I am suggesting is this:

We must recognize that in all effective communication, the emphasis should be on the receiver – the viewer, the listener or the reader. When we construct and deliver messages in any medium, we must develop them to fit and be appropriate for the receiver's abilities and expectations.

So, assume and expect quality. Don't aim for the lowest common denominator. Raise expectations, and aim for high quality.

When we produce and deliver quality products, services – and commercials – we are demonstrating a simple but very clear message to our present and potential customers.

We respect them. Demonstrating respect will go much further in business than going for a quick laugh.

And always remember this. Audiences may forget precisely what we say to them, but they will always remember how we make them feel."

Customer Service – Easy But Powerful

With apologies to Charles Dickens, I submit to you *Customer Service Tales from Two Cities*. I think the tales will demonstrate how easy it is to provide good customer service – as well as bad customer service.

Whether good or bad, we all remember how we are treated, and we tell others about our experiences. Word-of-mouth comments about a business are always more powerful than any other form of advertising.

That old adage states, "We may forget exactly what others do, and we may forget precisely what they say, but we never forget how they make us feel."

Feelings drive behavior.

How we make our customers feel will keep them coming to us, or it will drive them away.

Consider these two tales.

Tale Number 1. Late one afternoon, I checked into a hotel during a business trip.

The hotel didn't have a full restaurant, so on the way out, I stopped at the front desk and asked to change a one-hundred-dollar bill. I wanted smaller bills to use at a local fast food eatery.

The desk clerk said, "No. We don't make change."

I said, "I didn't walk in off the street. I'm a registered guest. You checked me in 30 minutes ago."

She said again, "We don't make change. That's our policy."

End of comment.

I took four steps to a nearby cooler, took out a two-dollar bottle of water, and paid for it with the hundred-dollar bill. The clerk gave me ninety-eight dollars in change!

I said, "Isn't this foolish? You wouldn't make change, but you accepted the bill for the purchase."

Her answer: "Requesting the change was asking for a favor. We don't do that. Purchasing the water was a business transaction."

How's that for customer service?

If I had thought fast enough, I would have returned the bottle of water and asked for a two dollar refund.

I wonder how she would have responded to that.

Tale Number 2. When my wife and I went to a restaurant in Georgia we were pleasantly surprised at the attention and quality of service we received from the wait staff. It was a rather large restaurant and filled to capacity, but managers stopped by and visited. They didn't just walk past and ask the usual, "How's everything?"

When we told them it was our first visit to the restaurant, they asked why we were in town, how long we would be there, why we selected the restaurant, where we lived, would we be back, etc. A pleasant, brief conversation. When dinner was finished, the waiter and the manager came to the table with a huge desert – complimentary. "This is to welcome you on your first visit. Thanks for coming. We hope you'll be back again."

That gesture was a complete surprise, totally unexpected, and completely unnecessary. They had no assurance we would ever return, because it isn't a resort or tourist location. Our trip was strictly business. Yet they honored our visit and expressed appreciation. They didn't have to do that, but they did.

How's that for customer service?

Coincidently, we were in that city for another business trip later that month. I'm sure you can guess which restaurant was high on our list.

In both instances the respective behavior was easy for the participants.

But the opposite behavior would have been easy, too. The desk clerk could have provided the change with no effort.

The waiter and manager could have withheld the unexpected desert and simply said, "Thank you for coming." The dining experience would have still been pleasant and memorable.

In every business, person-to-person thoughtfulness and consideration go a long way. In both tales, the people involved had a profound impact on how we feel about the respective businesses and the probability of doing repeat business with them.

It could be a good idea to think about how we make our customers feel – and why.

Speak Up – Don't Just Leave.

Have you ever been to a restaurant and found the meal you ordered wasn't up to the usual standards of the facility? Have you ever received "attitude" from a staff person when you requested assistance or information? What did you do?

Because most of us don't like confrontation, we just "make a face" or a noise, and we leave. That seems to make sense because we have many businesses from which to choose the next time, and we don't want to subject ourselves to such behavior again.

Here's something else to consider. When a dissatisfied customer simply leaves the premises, the business owner has no idea what happened. There is no way for the owner to know he or she might have a problem. The unsatisfactory food or service could prevent a return visit, and a potential long-time customer might be lost to the competition. When you are the customer in such a situation, tell whoever is in charge what went wrong. This isn't a "complaint." It's information. Further, it's a favor because now the owner can take steps to fix the shortcoming.

Here are a couple of examples. The first happened in a popular restaurant. A couple ordered the appetizer they had enjoyed many times before. When it was served, it was tough and very unpleasant. Not at all like their previous experiences.

They informed the manager calmly and pleasantly, and it was replaced. However, the replacement was the same as the original. When they returned the second order, the manager said they had just changed suppliers, and that very well could have been the cause of the change in quality.

Now the manager had feedback and could take immediate action. Without the customer comments, he would not have checked on the new supplier and taken corrective action.

The second example is a personal one. On a recent business trip I checked into a hotel close to the airport. I had never used the hotel before and needed information about their services.

This is when "attitude" began. I asked the desk clerk about the shuttle service schedule to get to my meeting site. She pointed to a little poster and said, "Everything is over there." No assist – just a point. When I understood the schedule, I asked her if I needed to make a reservation. That's necessary in many hotels I've stayed in before.

She answered, "It's complimentary."

My response, "That's good, but do I have to make a reservation?"

She replied, a little crisply, "It's complimentary!"

I continued, "Fine, but you're not answering my question."

Now came the attitude. She held up three fingers and said, "I answered that question three times. Now do you have any other questions?"

I asked for her name. There are dozens of hotels in that immediate area, and competition is fierce. The front desk clerk is the face of a hotel, and her attitude did nothing to encourage another stay – ever. I called the general manager to tell him how guests were being "welcomed."

He was disturbed, and he asked me for details. After a talk with the desk clerk, he called me back. Not surprisingly, her version of the conversation was different from mine.

I have no idea what subsequent action was taken, but I do know the manager was bothered by the image his desk clerk presented. His words to me were, "We can't have that. It will be addressed quickly. Thank you for the information." He was well aware of the importance of first impressions in assuring future business in a very competitive business,

Years ago, in an HR office, I saw a motivation poster, many of which are rather simplistic and trite, but this was a good one. The desk clerk encounter reminded me of that poster, and I think the hotel manager lives its message, as we all should. Here it is.

"If we don't take care of our customers, our competitors will."

Enough said.

CHAPTER 7

Interviewing

How others see us "perform" will usually influence how they think of us and if they will follow – or reject – our examples. What we "do" pulls them up –or down – to our standard. Don't take a chance with that standard.

Sooner or later every one of us is involved in an interview. We might be the interviewer, or we might be the one being interviewed. The circumstances might be job hunting or responding to news requests. It might be a tele-conference or a Skype discussion. Whatever the reason, what we do and what we say will be significant to a viewing or reading audience.

Many people do poorly in interviews because they think they can just "wing it" since they are the focus, and they have all the information.

That's a bad strategy.

It's essential to plan and prepare for an interview regardless of which side of the table you occupy. We create impressions during interviews, and it's important to create positive ones. Our futures often depend on how well or how poorly we perform when we are on the "hot seat."

This section illustrates how people have prepared, performed, and created impressions. It covers a variety of situations and outcomes, and contains examples of many techniques that worked well – or failed horribly.

Interrogation or Conversation?

An interview is a straightforward method of gathering information in order to form an opinion or make a decision. Most of us have gone through the process in order to gain admission to a school or to secure a job. Generally speaking, people often consider the event as uncomfortable, maybe intimidating, even frightening. The reason behind such feelings usually stems from unfamiliarity or lack of preparation. Let's look at how we can improve performance leading to confidence when faced with the academic and job search interview.

The overwhelming concept here is the belief one must be ready to answer many questions that come. The interviewer is the person in charge of the conversation and will lead the discussion by asking the questions. That is partly true, but if you keep the following fact in mind, interviews will be easier and you'll be more effective and successful.

Interviews are conversations!

That means both parties are equal players as far as the information exchange is concerned. Certainly, the interviewer will decide about admission or hiring, but that will be done on the basis of the information you provide. A candidate knows much more about his or her interests, experiences, goals, passions, talents, and abilities than the interviewer does.

Keeping that in mind, it's easy to see that the candidate must be the one to identify pertinent topics and experiences.

So, Rule Number One to follow in preparing for an interview is this: Determine what you want to say as well as refining responses to what the interviewer might ask. That two-pronged strategy is what will drive the "conversation."

I thought about this some time ago when I met a man who had been unsuccessful in a job search in which I participated. He said to me, "I thought my previous experience with sales at Company X would have been exactly what you were looking for."

I said, "You never mentioned doing any of that."

He said, "You didn't ask me."

I didn't respond out loud, but I found myself thinking, "How could I ask you anything about it if I didn't know about it?"

Now, let's set up the scenario to demonstrate how this works. Because there are many interview styles, we can't cover them all, but here's a pretty good overview.

The interviewer opens with, "I've read your application and resume, but tell me about yourself." This is a potential home run. What will you say? The interviewer will probably have a follow-up to your response as well as a set of prepared questions.

So, here's the next important step – Rule number 2. Answer every question, of course. If you don't, you'll be seen as evasive, uninformed, or incapable. But, don't stop there. Don't simply answer and wait for the next question to come at you. Remember – Conversation! As often and wherever possible at the end of your answer, bridge to a topic of your choice. This isn't changing the subject or avoiding an issue, it's expanding or illustrating your knowledge of and experience with the topic.

Here are some examples of "bridging statements" to use to make the transition from the answer to the experience:

"That's why I decided to…"

"Let me give you an example of how I…"

"That brings up the issue of…"

"Another way to look at that is…"

Add your own, and see how you can modify the direction of the conversation in order to assure you cover and display what is important from your perspective. In all likelihood, the interviewer will ask you a follow-up question about your comment, and you'll be in charge of the conversation. When you do that, the interviewer will see you as someone who can contribute to the institution and who can make an important contribution.

The same "conversation" system applies to interviews with the media: radio, television, or print.

Same basics, but with a few added nuances.

If You're Asking a Question, Don't Give a Speech.

I'm not sure if a trend is developing or if I'm just becoming aware of something that has existed for a long time. It relates to the way people ask questions. I've noticed this technique in corporate interviews and on radio and television news programs.

Let's start with the television news program for an example. A male host on one of the early morning talk shows – no need to name names, you'll find him if you want – almost always uses the following technique when he conducts interviews. He will say to the guest some-thing like, "You have said you believe we should blah, blah, blah, blah. Right?" He makes a little speech stating his own belief or interpretation and simply asks the guest to confirm what he said. His only question is, "Right?" The guest might say more, but the response is usually a limited one.

This technique enables the host to not only set the agenda and direction for the interview/conversation, but also to predetermine the direction of the answers. He states his bias or belief and asks only for confirmation. At other times he recites facts, numbers, and positions in a way that demonstrates how informed he is on a subject and then asks only for agreement from the guest by again asking, "Right?" When all he asks for is confirmation of his own ideas, he limits the response and risks missing the important facts and interpretations his guest might otherwise have provided.

I've seen this same technique used by Human Re-source staff when conducting interviews and by training personnel when running in-house classes. While the tech-nique might be comfortable for the "asker," it doesn't en-courage the full participation of the "answerer." When you ask a question, the idea is to get the other person to open up and provide his or her opinions and perceptions not simply to confirm yours. Further, when you control and limit the questions this way, the response very likely will be what the "answerer" thinks you want to hear ra-ther than what he actually believes. So you get inaccurate and, therefore, unreliable information. You lose an oppor-tunity.

Many of us have had to interview prospective or cur-rent employees whether we are in an HR Department or following up on a candidate HR has already screened. What we want to find out is what the candidate knows, has done, will do, and how well he'll fit into our organization. We can learn about those factors only by getting the candidate to talk freely and engage in a conversation, not just by answering our pointed questions and confirming our assumptions. People talk in response to those "open" questions we all know about but sometimes forget in the middle of an interview or conversation. "What," "Why," and "How" will provide you with a lot more information than you'll ever get from "Did," "Can," and "Will."

Once the conversation begins in response to a good opening question, keep it going. Prompt the candidate to continue talking and providing additional information with statements like, "Give me an example," or "Please be a little more specific," or "What else should I know?" Using these last three statements will encourage the candidate to participate in the conversation and to select what he or she sees as important and significant. The candidate will identify the examples that are relevant and the specific facts that support a stated position. When you open the conversation floodgates with that last line, "What else should I know?" the candidate will pick the area and the content, and you can learn a great deal. Often, what the candidate selects and talks about would never occur to you to ask. You may now have a brand new direction to pursue, one that might make the difference between a positive and a negative decision about hiring the candidate.

Exactly the same technique will work with current employees when you find it necessary to evaluate someone for a promotion or a transfer. This will get the other person talking, but now be sure you listen. It is only through an extended give-and-take conversation that you can identify the specific areas of interest and the abilities of a candidate or employee.

If you haven't conducted interviews this way in the past, try it. If you have done them this way, I'm sure you discovered you get more valuable information from a conversation than from an interrogation. Right?

(Just kidding!)

Interviews – Tell *Your* Story.

Have you ever been scheduled for an "interview" and felt panic, shakes, and a mental vacuum? You're not alone. That's typically what many people experience.

But it doesn't have to happen. Here's a plan that will help.

First, change how you feel about an interview. Look at it as an opportunity to be embraced, not as an obstacle to be avoided. That attitude shift alone is a helpful first step. Remember, when someone interviews you, it's because you have information that other person doesn't have – and wants.

Begin your preparation by determining what that person might ask you. Write down possible questions, and ask colleagues for their ideas too. If there's a Corporate Communications Department in your company, by all means, seek out their help and input right away. They know the reporters' reputations, interests, and possibly, their biases. Once you have an idea of what the reporter might be looking for, you're ready for the next step.

By the way, don't rely completely on what the reporter tells you he or she plans to ask. The actual interview might cover different material, not because the reporter is dishonest or devious, but because conditions could change between scheduling the interview and the actual event. Be ready for surprises.

Decide what *You* want to say. An interview is a conversation, not an interrogation. In every interview, there are two agendas present – the reporter's and yours. The reporter's agenda is to get a good story. Your agenda is to be a good spokesperson for your business and your company. Don't expect the reporter to tell your story. Tell it yourself.

Here's an example of how a good opportunity can be lost. A few years ago I was hosting a weekly thirty-minute radio talk program designed to showcase individuals and their businesses. The programs were typically recorded for later broadcasting. At the conclusion of one particular program that I thought went well I said to the guest, "That was good – very interesting."

He said, "Thanks, but we never got to talk about our new electronics venture."

"Why didn't you bring it up?" I asked.

"You didn't ask me about it." was his response.

"Sorry, but how could I? I didn't know about it," was my reply.

End of discussion.

Clearly, he lost an opportunity to talk about an interesting new corporate activity. He wasn't really engaged in a conversation. In his mind, this was a question-answer activity.

He waited for a question that never came because I didn't have any information about the new electronics.

I couldn't ask about something I didn't know existed. We couldn't re-do the program, so he missed a chance of getting free publicity for his company and its new venture.

Don't do the same thing when you are interviewed. During the conversation be sure to answer the questions the reporter asks, but don't stop there. Expand your answers and "bridge" to your point.

That's what my guest should have done. That's how you get to tell *Your* story.

Do that by using statements like these to get from the answer to a question to what you want to say: "That's precisely why we are introducing our new…" "That's why it's important to recognize that…" "I think your question is really about…" "Another way to look at that is…" "If we take a step back, we can see the larger issue is…"

This technique will help you make your point and contribute to producing an interesting program. Both you and the reporter win, and that always makes for a good interview.

Here's one final point about interviews and their value to you and your company. Think of interviews as free advertising.

The interview is a chance to inform the public, and possibly new customers, about what you're doing, how you're doing it, and why it's good.

That's what the advertising department pays for, but you get to do it at no cost.

As with a good commercial, tell the audience what you want them to know.

Think about what it would cost to purchase 2-4 minutes of airtime to run a commercial spot. You're getting it at no cost through the interview, so use the time and the opportunity to your advantage.

Finally, here's a question that is often asked, and it provides the chance to soar if you answer well or sink if you don't, "What else should I know about your company?"

Always be ready for it so you don't miss a big opportunity.

When it comes at you, what will you say?

Face-to-Face Interviews

In a previous section, we suggested techniques to use when being interviewed via telephone for a job or college admission. In this section, we'll discuss factors related to face-to-face interviews. Content, of course, is of paramount importance so be sure to "tell your story" during the interview. Don't just answer questions, though, because an interview should be a two-way conversation.

Before the interview, determine what points you want to make. Say them out loud, but don't memorize them. The practice will enable you to make those points clearly and concisely during the interview. Don't limit your planning to only the content. There are other factors to control, and they can make or break the impression you want to create.

Those factors include two specific items: how you look, and what you do. You'll certainly have a good handle on the verbal content, but behavioral psychologists estimate that between 60 and 80% of communication is non-verbal. During the interview you'll be sending many non-verbal signals so it's important to know what they are. Then, whatever you do - do it on purpose. Control your behavior, and you'll create the perceptions you want others to have of you.

Judging begins the instant you meet the interviewer. In his book, *You Are the Message*, Roger Ailes wrote, "You have only six seconds to make a first impression."

Connect with the interviewer immediately, or your quest might be over quickly. A motion picture director once told me, "When I'm holding auditions, as soon as I meet an actor, I find myself deciding whether or not I want to spend much time with him." (In the movie business, by the way, both males and females are referred to as actors.) He continued, "It might not be fair, but that's what happens. I'm always polite and provide the opportunity for the actor to read for the part, but that first impression is powerful. Sometimes an actor's subsequent behavior might change my mind, but that's rare."

The behavioral psychologists also tell us that most people put little or no thought into the messages their bodies send. So what can you do to start your interview on a positive note that will create the impression you want?

When you enter the interview room: Stand tall (as tall as you can, no matter your actual height). Shake hands (base of your thumb to the base of the interviewer's thumb). Grasp firmly (but this isn't a strength contest). Speak with a full voice (no whispering and no shouting). Look him in the eye (essential in the Western world). Hold your chin up (shows confidence). But don't stick it out (that's arrogance).

When you're invited to sit: Sit up straight (like your mother said). Lean slightly forward, feet on the floor. Sit still. Many chairs rock, roll, swivel, and tilt. Keeping your feet planted will keep you steady, and you'll look calm and comfortable (even if you don't feel that way).

Your gestures should match your words. Let your hands show, "big, small, up, down, high, low, etc." Don't fold them on your lap or clasp them tightly on the tabletop. Use them.

Although some people might advise you otherwise, avoid the temptation to "mirror" the interviewer. He isn't being evaluated for a position, you are. Be yourself, not a mirror image of someone else.

Take your time when talking. Give yourself time to take a breath. If you talk fast, you'll risk misspeaking, stumbling, and filling the conversation with annoying non-words like um, ah, ya'know, etc. Talking fast usually connotes nervousness – not what you want to convey.

Finally, if you have papers or other items you intend to show during the interview, be sure you know exactly where they are in your briefcase so you won't struggle to find them.

Remember the importance of those first few seconds. Rehearse these skills and you'll get started well. Once you've created that initial impression, the rest will get easier.

Hunting for a Job?

Employment numbers vary from time to time during the year like increasing because schools let out for the summer and a new wave of graduates joins the work force. Job-hunting is a difficult process. Sometimes it's a bit overwhelming. The search requires patience and resolve, but sooner or later a possibility presents itself.

At that point, many applicants stumble because they don't do well with the interview. Candidates need to learn how to navigate an interview. I use the word "navigate" because, as with taking a trip by car, boat, or plane, it requires preparation. We must "plot a course." To do that we must know two things: where we are, and where we want to go. The "where we are" part of the interview includes information about the candidate including skills, experience, expectations, intentions, and accomplishments. The "where we want to go" part of an interview is displaying real interest in getting the job and expanding career opportunities in the future.

Let's look at the preparation aspect first. Then we'll explore the interview, and finally the wrap-up. Many of the steps will seem obvious when first mentioned, but all too often candidates overlook the obvious. Here's the sequence. Anticipate questions to give yourself guidance. Don't just think about the questions, write them down. If you don't write them, you can't be sure what they are and how you'll answer them.

You're selling yourself to a customer – the interviewer – and you want him or her to "buy you." What does the interviewer need to know to make a good decision? Ask yourself: What can I do? What have I already done? What do I want to do? Be specific! Indicating a desire "to make the world a better place by working for universal peace" is nice, but it's fluff. It says nothing about your ability or accomplishments. Don't wait for the interviewer to ask questions – take the initiative. You know more about you than anyone else. Many people are hesitant to talk about themselves because they feel it comes across as self-serving or bragging. Remember this old adage: "It ain't bragging, if you can do it."

Also, be prepared to ask the interviewer questions about the job and the company. Remember, an interview is a conversation – not an interrogation. If you're eventually offered a position you want to know what kind of organization you'll be joining. It seems impossible to imagine candidates making errors in the following areas. They do. Show up on time.

Dress appropriately. If you're not sure how employees dress, over-dress. You can always remove a jacket or a tie, but it's hard to cover up gym shoes and T-shirts.

Don't take or make cell phone calls before or during your interview time. Put on your professional "game face" and demeanor as soon as you enter the building. Keep it on until you're outside again. You never know who or where the interviewer will be, so be sure you appear positive and professional at all times.

If you are inclined – or addicted – to informing the world about yourself on social media – don't! At least, be careful. What you post in jest might revisit you in an interview.

Finally, ask for the job if you want it. Don't be coy or subtle when it's so easy and productive to say, "I want to work here because…"

If everything works out well, and you're offered and you accept a position, ask about the next steps. What will the employer do, and what should you do? In all walks of life, planning must precede execution to assure a positive outcome.

A former colleague of mine told me this story about preparation. When he was teaching at a major university he encountered a student exiting a campus chapel. The student told Jack he had a big test coming up later in the day and stopped to say a prayer.

"That's good," said Jack, "but did you study?"

CHAPTER 8

Interpersonal Communication

No one knows how anyone else actually feels about anything. But everyone makes judgments about others. We do that on the basis of what those others say and what they do. It's behavior that counts.

For most of us, our behaviors are monitored and evaluated whether we know it or like it. So, it's in our own best interest to be aware of what we do and how we do it. Always remember: Whatever you do – do it on purpose.

Words, gestures, posture, and movement all contribute to what others think, and every one of those behaviors can and should be purposeful. Not only do others judge us, we judge them, too.

This section reflects a wide variety of behaviors that have worked for or against people in business and civic situations. Some of the instances are frivolous, some are serious, but they all show how individual behaviors influ-

ence perceptions. The techniques explored and the anecdotes recounted will help avoid missteps.

Attitude Is A State of Mind.

The way we manage a business, a department, or a
service depends on the attitude, the frame of mind that we
bring to the situation. We are our own supporters or our
own adversaries when it comes to creating that frame of
mind.

I used the word "creating" attitudes deliberately because that's exactly what we do - either consciously or
unconsciously. We form our attitudes. They don't just
happen. In our book, *Becoming a Successful Manager*,
my colleague, Jack Grossman, and I defined attitude this
way. "It is a state of mind and a predisposition to action
based on what you tell yourself."

This is an important concept in business because
what we tell ourselves determines how we will behave
and how we will communicate with others around us. For
example, if we look to find fault, we'll certainly find it.
If, on the other hand, we look for positive actions, we'll
find those, too. And we do this to ourselves with great
regularity even though we aren't aware we are doing it.
Here's a simple example.

Think of a time you were going to a dinner party and
were certain you would have an unpleasant time when
you got there. Chances are excellent you were right about
it. You did have an unpleasant time. You knew you
should have stayed home. For the sake of everyone else
at that dinner party, maybe you should have.

You told yourself you wouldn't enjoy the event, and
you didn't. If, on the other hand, you had expected a

pleasant evening and told that to yourself, you probably enjoyed the party.

Now, let's put this into business. Think of a situation in which you told yourself you looked forward to a meeting or to delivering a presentation. Most likely you entered into the activity with that positive attitude, and you probably did well. Your frame of mind determines your behavior, and your behavior will result in a reaction from those with whom you come in contact. Here's a specific situation we described in our book which supports the idea of attitude influencing behavior. Customer service representatives at a particular company were performing poorly when answering the phone. Obviously, that was the major part of their jobs. Customer complaints increased, and this company faced serious difficulties. By the way they answered the phone, the customer service representatives communicated that they didn't want to help the callers. This wasn't a conscious decision on their part, of course, it just seemed to happen.

We made this suggestion to all the customer service representatives. Before you answer the phone ask yourself, "How can I help this person? He or she is calling because something is wrong, and I have the ability to fix it." They all tried this, and service improved. The only difference was what the representatives told themselves, but the changes were dramatic.

Here are a couple of areas in which you might try this attitude observation and improvement. The next time you attend a corporate training program tell yourself you're looking forward to learning something. You probably will! Many busy business people attend such programs and expect them to be a waste of time. Usually they prove themselves correct, not because of the content or the method of delivery of the program but because that's what they told themselves.

Finally, for practice, listen to the way the company receptionist greets callers and visitors. This is often the first contact people have with your company. Does the receptionist convey clearly a desire to help or to put up obstacles? It's easy to do either one of those, but it requires a conscious effort. Like so many other behaviors, this is a skill we need to develop and practice. As with other skills, the more we practice, the better we'll do.

Since our relationships with clients, customers, and colleagues is so important to the success of our businesses, this new skill is well worth the effort it takes to perfect it.

Cell Phones and Common Consideration

As cell phones have become smaller, users are talking louder. When first introduced, cell phones were big, heavy, and clumsy. And they were all gray – no designer colors. I still have the first Motorola "brick" I purchased many years ago, but its function now is serving as a bookend holding information in place on my bookcase rather than transmitting it through cyberspace. In the old cell phones, the earpiece and the microphone were located approximately where a user's ear and mouth are positioned so no one felt the need to project loudly to be heard. Cell phone conversations were controlled and somewhat private.

All that has changed. The microphone is now positioned near the user's ear, but it is sensitive enough to pick up the voice without adding volume. For most users, however, it doesn't feel that way so the small phones encourage louder voices. Now, that alone wouldn't be too bad if the only listener was the person on the other end of the phone conversation. Unfortunately, many other inno-cent bystanders are subjected to the thoughts and voices of the user. It seems that, no matter where we are these days, at meetings, in elevators, restaurants, hallways, even rest rooms, we are the unwilling recipients of infor-mation we don't need, don't want, or don't deserve. We just can't get away from those loud, inconsiderate talkers.

Cell phones are absolutely essential in business these days, but it is important for all of us to be aware of others around us. They aren't interested in being part of our conversations, so let's not force ourselves on them. There are many ways to accomplish that. The easiest actions, of course, are to pick a more private location for a call and turn down our volume.

Everyone around us will appreciate such thoughtful-ness.

Here's another way I witnessed recently, a way that was effective although it required a good bit of risk. I don't recommend it, but it's a good story, and it makes a point. Here's what happened.

Passengers were seated on a plane but take-off was delayed, and the pilot announced it would be okay to use cell phones while we waited. Many passengers just groaned or rolled their eyes at another flight delay, but the passenger in the window seat in the aisle ahead of mine made a phone call. Everyone around him was sub-jected to his end of the conversation because we were trapped.

After a few minutes of the loud talk, the man in the aisle seat next to the caller became a bit annoyed at the loud talk.

He took a pad and pen out of his briefcase and turned toward the caller. And he began to take notes on what he heard. Soon the caller realized what was happening and said, "What are you doing?"

The note-taker replied, "You were talking so loudly, I assumed what you were saying was important, and you wanted everyone to pay attention. I didn't want to miss anything."

The man in the window seat looked angry, but he ended the call, turned his back on the note-taker, looked out the window, and didn't say another word during the two and a half hour flight.

Obviously, there could have been many other, less benign reactions, but that was the end of this encounter. Don't try it yourself, but enjoy the story.

The lesson, however, is clear. Others near us don't want and don't need to hear our phone conversations. Spare them that.

The small cell phone instruments are very sensitive and don't require loud voices. For private conversations, find a private location.

To borrow and distort a little bit of Teddy Roosevelt, "Talk softly…" Forget the big stick, and remember your immediate neighbors. Respect the person on the other end of your phone call, but also respect those near you. Privacy is important for all parties. Honor it.

There is one other reason for silence. Because business phone calls often include privileged information, in the heat of discussion you might say something you didn't intend.

Once said, it cannot be retrieved, and you don't know who might overhear your comments. Don't contribute to inappropriate corporate misspeak.

In all matters of media use, be sure you control the technology.

Don't let the hardware or the software influence your behavior because others won't evaluate the tools you use.

They'll evaluate you.

We Miss You Most When You're Home.

In this segment we're going to take a slightly different view of business communications. In the past we've concentrated only on what we do on the job, but there is another very important part of our business lives, and that's the effect our actions can have on our personal lives.

With only a limited amount of time available to us, we have to juggle a variety of priorities. Business pressures, social pressures, and family pressures all seem to close in on us at the same time.

Sometimes those priorities might be misplaced.

I want to tell you a brief story which demonstrates conflicting priorities, and I invite you to consider how you might respond in a situation such as this one.

A few years ago, I was working with a group of very successful executives. At one of our regular meetings, the discussion turned to family responsibilities and the pressures of business travel. Everyone agreed travel was difficult, but it was necessary. It was certainly an important part of their success.

One of the men, Steve, brought us all up short and changed the course of the discussion with this story.

He had returned home from an "important" business trip one Friday evening and spent most of the day Saturday doing the paperwork required to close out the trip.

On Sunday he began packing his suitcase and briefcase for the coming week when his seven-year-old son asked him to play catch with him in the backyard.

Steve explained he couldn't play because he had to get ready for the upcoming trip. Tommy's shoulders dropped.

Seeing that the little boy was disappointed, Steve stopped packing and said to him, "Tommy, you know I have to take these trips, even though I don't want to. And you know how much I miss you and Mom when I'm away."

Tommy just stood there for a moment. He knew there would be no game of catch – again. Steve was too busy for that. With a little tear in his eye, Tommy said, "I know you miss us, Dad, and we miss you, too, when you're away. But we miss you most when you're home."

The meeting room got very quiet as we all thought about our personal family lives. There aren't any simple or uncomplicated decisions for many of the situations we face, but it's probably a good idea for all of us to evaluate our priorities and think of the considerable impact we have on the lives of those around us as we go about our daily schedule.

Now let's look at that business schedule and see how the story relates to what we do on the job. Think about how often we get caught up in our activities and forget that others have their own priorities too. And those are just as pressing and just as important as ours. A basic tenant of business is the need to build relationships – with customers, colleagues, co-workers, and the people who report to us.

Building relationships requires operating on a two way street. We have to let people know how we feel and what we think is important. That's one side of the street. The other side is when and how we observe and listen to others, and find out how they feel and what they think is important.

Effective business speech goes both ways. Here's a little exercise you might find useful. For the next week or so pay close attention to how often and how long you do most of the talking when you're on the job.

At the same time, track how often and for how long you listen to others. If you're not listening and observing enough maybe you'll miss important information available from those around you.

In order to be successful it's important for us to build positive business relationships, and that happens only when we are aware of what others around us need, want, and deserve.

Don't give just directions and commands. Give time and attention too.

None of us would want our colleagues to paraphrase Steve's son, Tommy, and say to us, "We miss you most when you're here on the job."

CHAPTER 9

Selling Skills

Most people think the be all and end all of business is selling products and service. That's not accurate. Certainly currency and valuables change hands and ownership within the selling encounter, but—"Selling" isn't the operative word. In fact, in a study done many years ago researches asked both salespeople and customers about the sales interaction. One of the questions was, "What bothers you most about salespeople?" Both the salespeople and the customers gave the same answer: "Salespeople talk too much!"

The consensus was salespeople would be more successful and more effective if they asked questions and then listened to the answers. That way they would have the information to get the customer to buy whatever they were offering. So concentrating on "buying" is more significant and productive than focusing on "selling" in the sales setting.

Here are tales of good sales techniques and bad ones.

What is most interesting is that whenever anyone examines these encounters it's easy to detect the errors. The big question then is, "Why do so many salespeople get it wrong?

What Does Your Customer Need?

The key to a successful sales meeting isn't the selling part, it's the buying part. Because there is so much to discuss during a sales call, it's easy to forget items that could be helpful. Here's a sequence that will help move the call to a successful conclusion.

First of all, think of a sales call as a two-way conversation not as a one-way presentation. Of course, eventually there will be a specific recommendation to purchase a product or service, but in the early stages of the interaction work to get the customer to talk. This will differentiate you from your competition because most customers are used to being told something, not being asked something. After you've learned what is important to the customer, build a relevant proposal detailing how you can meet that need.

Here's a seven-step process to gather the information while staying focused and on target. Use these prompts to help the customer tell you what is important.

Present conditions? Even before the sales call begins, get to know as much as you can about the client and the company he represents. Use the electronic media: Facebook, Google, etc. Talk to your colleagues who have had contact with the business, read annual reports and newspaper stories about the company. Identify relevant successes, failures, and aspirations.

Future conditions? What does the company want to

accomplish in the coming years? Some of that information will come through the research material above. But remember, companies don't buy things – people do. Find out what is important to the person. Is it Job Security? Establishing a reputation? Avoiding a transfer? That person is going to make a purchase decision that will affect you, so be sure to learn all you can about the individual.

Barriers? What could be in the way of "doing a deal?" Budget? Personnel? Timetable? Physical factors? Authority? In other words, are you talking to the right person?

Drivers? Find out why the client agreed to meet with you. Is he looking to get a promotion, a different assignment, save his current job? Is there some way doing business with you might help achieve that goal?

Support? Is there sufficient interest in working with you? Does the company have sufficient resources? Will your product or service fit into the client's budget, time frame, priority listing? Is there sufficient interest or need in the client's organization to justify spending money with you?

Collecting this information requires listening carefully to the client. Clients may freely offer specifics or you might have to ask specific questions. Either way, you'll need the information before making an appropriate recommendation. That's the reasoning behind describing the sales meeting as a "discussion," rather than as a presentation. In time, you'll make a "sales pitch," but it will flow smoothly as a way to help the client achieve what he or she needs – not simply as a way for you to make a sale.

Benefit Connection? You know what you can offer, and throughout the discussion you'll find the link between the customer's needs and your capabilities. Describe that linkage to the client, and describe the benefits of the connection. The more overlap between the client's needs and your offerings, the stronger the probability of making a sale.

Transition? When you have secured all the information you need, and the time comes to offer your product or service, shift from listening to the client to making your sales presentation by using this transition sentence, "Based on what you told me, here's what we can do."

The impression is you're helping the client acquire what he needs to do his job. People buy from people – not from companies. They buy from someone who can help them achieve their goals. Using this "discussion" technique also will help you achieve your own sales goals.

Everyone wins.

R.E.V. Up Your Sales Sequence.

Have you ever wondered why selling is such a difficult, and sometimes, unpleasant task? Successful business requires us to sell our products and services, but sometimes we fall into a behavior pattern which is less than positive. Much of what we do, we do by habit. If the habit results in what we want, fine. If, however, the habit doesn't result in what we want, we should change the habit. Easier said than done, so let me suggest a way to do it.

First, change your point of view. Don't focus on "selling" because that's only half of the equation. Focus on "buying." Buying is the operative behavior in any sales encounter. We can "sell up a storm," but if a customer doesn't buy, all is for naught. If you present a product or service in a way that fits a customer's needs or requirements, the eventual sale will be more likely. So find out what your customer needs or wants to buy before making your sales presentation.

Here's a way to do that. R.E.V. up your sales sequence. The letters strand for Ready, Encourage, and Value. Think of sales as a conversation – not as a "pitch." Both parties in any conversation should be equally involved, but often it's difficult to get a customer to talk. Sales people then fill up the silence, and they talk too much. Because the customer doesn't have his chance to talk, he often breaks away from the encounter, and the potential sale goes with him.

Design the sales conversation using a 3-step sequence. For illustration, I'll suggest some specific language, but use words that work for you and flow easily, but be sure to use this sequence.

Begin with, "I'm *Ready* to discuss our new product line, but first…" This leads to the second step. *Encourage* the customer to talk. "Tell me what you're looking for." He knows more about what he needs and wants than you do, so let him tell you. The third step is pointing out the *Value* your product or service will provide. Now you're describing how you plan to help the customer make a good "buy" decision.

Putting it all together sounds like this. "I'm *Ready* to show you our new offerings, but before I do that please tell me what you're looking for. That way we can focus on what has the greatest value to you."

Quick and easy. You start the conversation by setting a collegial tone, encouraging the customer to offer immediate input, and then indicating why this is a good way for him to proceed. Both parties talk, listen, talk, listen, etc. This is a true conversation between equals.

Listen carefully to what the customer is telling you, Ask specific questions for clarification and expansion to

fully understand the customer's perspective and prefer-
ences.

You'll need this information because eventually
you'll shift into your sales presentation by saying this.
"Based on what you told me, here's what I recommend."
When the customer sees that the product or service you
recommend is based on what he said, he'll be more inclined to buy from you. He'll see you're not s*elling* a
thing. Rather he will be *buying* a solution.

Obviously, the customer makes the ultimate decision
about spending his money with you or with someone else,
but when a salesperson is perceived as helping a customer, the chances of a sale increase dramatically. The customer knows best what he wants. The salesperson knows
best what products, services, or options are available.
When a salesperson takes the time to listen, he can match
what he has with what the customer needs. The customer
then will be much more inclined to make the purchase.

We often hear that effective selling is all about building positive relationships. Encouraging a customer to
talk, listening to what he says, and recommending solutions based on his needs is precisely how relationships
are built. Customers don't buy things, they buy people.
Listening can make you a valuable and trusted partner in
a "buy-sell" relationship.

So R.E.V. up your sales sequence, and see what happens.

Selling Isn't the Operative Word.

A few years ago, a study was done to assess the relationship that existed between salespeople and those who
buy their products and services. Among the many ques-

tions, buyers were asked, "What bothers you most about salespeople?" More than half answered, "They talk too much."

The salespeople were then asked the same question, and surprisingly, their answer was, "They talk too much." The salespeople saw their behavior in precisely the same way the buyers saw it.

Why do salespeople talk too much? The answer has two parts. First, they know a great deal about their product or service, and second, they want to generate income. Let's look at both of these laudable goals. As for generating income, no one in business would ever object to that as long as the method and the offering are legal and ethical.

With product knowledge, here's the problem. Salespeople feel they must tell customers everything about their product. They can talk at great length because of their wealth of knowledge. Product knowledge is essential in order to survive and compete. A pen salesman, for example, knows all about his product so he can describe the manufacturing process, material components, and on, and on, and on.

However, if a customer doesn't need or want the product or service, that's the end of the conversation. If that pen salesman's customer, for example, needs something erasable, no sale will be made regardless of the volume of information delivered.

In selling, the operative word isn't selling, it's buying.

Until the customer buys, there is no closure. So it's essential for the salesperson to learn what the customer needs and wants before attempting to sell anything.

How can a salesperson do that? Simple. Ask the customer. Invite him to talk. Listen to what he says. Then base your sales presentation on that information.

With the pen salesman example, if the customer had been encouraged to describe what he needs in his business, the ability to erase errors would certainly come up quickly.

Armed with that information, the salesperson could adjust his presentation. If his product line included an erasable product, that's the one he would offer, and he wouldn't waste time describing something inappropriate. If the product line didn't include such an item he could conclude the call gracefully and move on to other customers.

That would use his time well, and it would demonstrate his respect for his customer's time by not discussing irrelevant items.

If you are a salesperson, try this sequence. Very early in the sales call, encourage your customer to talk by asking him to tell you what's important for him in conducting his business. Then listen to the answer.

This will immediately differentiate you from your competition in the customer's mind. Salespeople talk too much. When you listen to a customer, you demonstrate you value his input.

Encourage the customer to continue talking with comments like, "Tell me more about that." "How might that modify your business?"

After collecting such information from your customer, link your offerings to the customer's requirements. This is called a "benefit connection," and it demonstrates you're working to help the customer solve his problems, not just sell your product.

Most salespeople are pressed for time, and at first glance this suggestion might seem to use up valuable face time. Just the opposite happens. Most customers welcome the chance to describe what they need. If you can offer a product to meet that need, the customer will buy it.

Using a benefit connection, the customer sees the sales presentation being based on his needs and not on the listings in your catalogue.

It makes little difference if that customer is the buyer for a mega corporation or a walk-in to a local store.

You can usually learn what a customer wants if you just give him time to tell you.

Then he'll "buy" from you what you might not be able to "sell" to him.

CHAPTER 10

Civic / Public Service

Very often we simply rely on the comfort of old habits to determine how we behave toward others. Old habits "feel good."

That's why we repeat them over and over again.

Many people believe the old adage that states," Practice makes perfect."

That's not true!

If anyone practices doing something the wrong way, it never gets good. It just feels better doing it the wrong way.

The way we respond to our schools, our churches, and our government speaks loudly about us.

Do we help, or do we criticize?

Do we support or do we destroy?

It's easy to make those choices. But the consequences and the implications deserve careful and prior attention.

Here are some suggestions and examples.

P.C. + Zero Tolerance = Conflict

Here's a provocative thought: *Any positive behavior – when taken to an extreme – produces negative results.*

We know life will continue to be filled with highs and lows. We'll make numerous decisions about our businesses and our personal lives. And, we'll rely on a variety of guidelines and policies. Some of those guidelines, however, collide with each other. Good intentions become distorted, and they often result in contradictions and confusion. (You know what they say about good intentions.)

Two such guidelines, Political Correctness and Zero Tolerance are evident today in our businesses, our schools, our government, and our communities. Each one seemed to be a good idea when it first appeared on the American scene. PC was intended to be a way to protect individuals, their sensitivities, and their feelings. Zero Tolerance was intended to punish bad behavior swiftly and consistently.

With PC, the intention was to be sensitive to others – not inadvertently insulting or embarrassing anyone. No one would feel inferior to anyone else. Everyone would be equal. A nice thought, but it doesn't always work. Clearly, everyone is not equal to everyone else. We all have different strengths, weaknesses, interests, and talents. To think otherwise is naive.

Some of the people we hire in our businesses are better workers than others. Some of our customers are more astute than others. Some in each category are self-sufficient, but some need extra "tender loving care." Attempting to treat everyone and every situation in exactly the same way doesn't work. In fact it can lead to unequal treatment of individuals.

Here's an example. When kids play on a baseball

team, many adults have decided that no one should keep score so the poor players won't feel bad at the end of a game. No score – no losers. Seems okay. The only thing wrong with that is the fact that all the kids know who the good players are, who the bad players are, and who "won" the game.

The well-intentioned adults fool no one but themselves.

PC teaches a wrong lesson. Kids can't win or lose, but professional athletes are rewarded – or punished – on the basis of their performance. Those messages are in conflict. When employees are paid on the basis of their performance, some work hard to succeed, but some do the minimum. When everyone receives the same wage, performance and productivity often suffer. PC becomes a negative.

Zero Tolerance, likewise, leaves no room for mature judgment. In the Zero Tolerance world everything is either always good or always bad. Everything is either black or white. But life isn't like that. Common sense and experience tell us we live and work in worlds filled with shades of gray.

Zero Tolerance in the workplace – be it a store, a factory, the military, or a school – makes it easy for any manager to make decisions because he doesn't have to make any decisions.

All he or she has to do is follow blindly whatever a directive says without recognizing the circumstances and consequences that often influence actions. Zero Tolerance is actually an extremely weak way to manage any organization.

Recently, two news accounts demonstrated the contradictions associated with these two beliefs. The first relates to what happened at Fort Hood, Texas. Prior to the massacre, many people who knew Major Malik Nadal

Hasan neglected to comment on his behavior because such comments might "offend" Muslims. PC contributed to the murders of innocent people!

That same week, a young middle school student "poked" another student's knee with a pencil. He was immediately expelled because school leaders had defined the action as an attack with a weapon. Imagine that. A pencil in a school being defined as a weapon!

Zero Tolerance taken to an extreme!

Sensitivity and consistency certainly are positive behaviors, but taking them to the extremes described in these two scenarios became negatives. As managers, teachers, leaders, and administrators, we all have to make decisions every day. In life, there is no "one size fits all." Differences are what make life and business interesting, challenging, and frustrating, but also exciting and rewarding.

If we think carefully about how we conduct our daily activities we'll see the importance of avoiding extremes.

Think again about that opening comment: *Any positive behavior – when taken to an extreme – produces negative results.*

CHAPTER 11

Generational Differences

The world continues to change, but many business-people don't recognize the changes. It seems that people of all generations – and there are four distinctly different generations currently in the workforce – think their method of observation and activity is the only one.

At least they think it's the best one.

The fact is it's one of many, and to continue to be successful, all parties must know what "makes the other one tick."

The methods, expectations, and rewards of the four groups are all distinct. Whenever the composition of the groups changes, all parties must adjust. It's a never-ending process.

A plaque on a CEO's desk presented a startling prophecy many of his colleagues didn't even want to consider. Think about this message: "In one hundred years – all new people."

Multi-tasking By Any Other Name
Is Still Rude.

Many business people pride themselves on the ability to multi-task, to do two or more things at the same time. In fact they look forward to situations in which they can practice and demonstrate it. They wait on a customer and talk on the phone, or they stock shelves while assisting a shopper.

Teleconferences are ideal settings for multi-taskers. They enter a room when a meeting is already underway, and they immediately turn on their laptops, cell phones, and text devices. They are ready to take on the entire world and all it has to offer because multi-taskers believe they can participate in the designated meeting and engage in all of the other options simultaneously.

They're wrong.

They may be manipulating all of the technologies at the same time, but no one can devote 100 percent attention to more than one thing at a time. It's impossible. No one can listen, see, think, read, write, reflect, compute, etc. all at once. Even really "smart people" can't do all of that. They think they can, but, again, they're wrong. Something suffers.

We've all seen this many times when the multi-tasker asks questions that have already been asked – and answered, when they embark on issues that have absolutely nothing to do with the topic at hand, and/or when they introduce ideas that have nothing to do with the topic of a meeting.

In many respects, multi-taskers are just plain rude. They are more interested in what they want to do than in following the agenda of a meeting and contributing to its success.

Their multiple, simultaneous activities often disrupt

or detain discussions rather than supporting and directing them.

Recently I heard a new word to describe and justify multi-tasking. It's "switching," and it's defined – in a rather defensive way – as being very different from multi-tasking in this respect. While multi-tasking describes engaging in many activities simultaneously, switching describes giving complete attention to one thing – for a short period of time – and then redirecting that complete attention to something else.

Switching addresses the need to give full attention to looking, listening, or reading that are impossible with multi-tasking. Switchers feel they are, indeed, giving 100 percent attention to a topic. They just move quickly from topic to topic. That sounds good, but it doesn't work any better than multi-tasking.

When I was told about switching – by a switcher of course – I made this comparison to get a handle on the practice. While watching TV with a remote in hand, jumping from channel to channel might seem to be allowing a viewer to watch multiple programs at the same time.

It is possible to get the general sense of multiple programs, but often something significant is said or done on one channel after the viewer has moved to an alternate channel. It's easy to miss a touchdown or a hole in one, or to miss a significant sentence in a speech moments after moving to another channel. Even though the switcher is giving 100 percent attention to a specific topic or idea, other topics and ideas are being discussed on the other channels. And the switcher misses them.

Switching is an interesting concept, but no one can give full attention to something beyond his or her ability to perceive it. The take away from all of this is clear and simple. Concentrate fully on discussion topics. Be fully present at meetings. Colleagues and customers will notice and appreciate your consideration and attention.

Years ago I was given this piece of advice I think we all can use in our businesses. When talking to someone, look him or her in the eye. Pay complete attention. And tell yourself this, "At this moment, this person is the most important person in the world to me."

Others may be nearby, and other distractions might exist, but give full attention to the person and the topic at hand. You can move on to those other topics and people at a later time.

Do yourself, and others the favor of attention. Show respect for the time and interests of others.

Doing one thing at a time, and doing it well, will serve you well.

Celebrate the Differences

The workplace isn't necessarily an actual place anymore. Computer technology has expanded the reach of every business and of every customer. Effective communication requires that we consider the different audiences we face every day. Remember, communication is all about the audience. We've often been reminded of this basic principle. To be an effective presenter, you must think like your audience. So what do we know about the workforce population that constitutes our various audiences?

That population now includes four major groups: Traditionalists (born between 1927-1945), Baby Boomers (born between 1946-1964), Generation X (born between 1965-1980), and Generation Y (born after 1981). These aren't just labels. They include individuals with different work habits, expectations, and attitudes. The members of each group bring valuable contributions, but communicating effectively with them requires attention and flexibility.

How do you navigate a conversation among different people, for example, where some see technology as a simple convenience, others call it a complication, and still others see it as an integral way of life?

Consider the varied factors that might exist within your workforce. Traditionalists and early Baby Boomers grew up in an age of corporate structure, having to justify themselves, pay their dues, and bide their time. They are less tech-savvy than younger generations, and they prefer in-person interaction rather than e-mails and technological gadgets.

Late Baby Boomers, GenXers and GenYers (also known as Millennials) grew up in a more global economy filled with layoffs, downsizing, and off shoring. These relatively younger groups learned from the do-more-with-less mantra. GenYers often want only bits and pieces of information, specifically, the parts they feel are most important to them.

In some instances they are uncomfortable with face-to-face communication because of their extensive use of text messaging, cell phones, and e-mail.

They are used to working in a fast paced environment, but short, abrupt communication might omit important details.

The older generations, however, may over-inform causing confusion or the need to dig out the pertinent information.

GenYers are creative, optimistic, and tech-savvy. They act and react quickly. Traditionalists, on the other hand, prefer to build relationships over time. There is a great attitudinal and behavioral divide among these generations. Communicating with them as customers, colleagues and co-workers requires awareness, understanding, and a willingness to be flexible in the messages we send and the way we send them.

We can't expect a one-size-fits-all methodology to work today. It's important for all of us to become "multilingual" in the way we communicate. Since the most important element in the communication process is what the receiver thinks a message means, we must be sure messages are clear before sending them.

Here's an example of a perceived "clear" message that got lost. I once ordered a club sandwich *with mayo on the side.*

When the order arrived – with no mayo – I informed the waitress of the oversight. Indignantly, she pointed to the mayo carefully spread on the cut sides of each piece of bread, and said, "It's right there on the side." In her mind she delivered exactly what I had ordered!

Although this is a light-hearted example, consider for a moment how the four different groups might react when confronted with such a misunderstanding related to business topics.

What impact might their reactions have on future communication you might have with them?

When constructing messages, ask yourself these questions. What do I want to convey? Who's getting the information? What options do I have for sending it?

Evaluate those options, and choose what will work best. It doesn't matter which group you represent, being multi-lingual is important for members of all four groups. No one method of communication is better than another. Each is simply different – and so are the people who receive your messages.

Recognize those differences and celebrate them.

Social Media Ain't Very Sociable.

Have you ever wondered why you didn't get called for a job or admissions interview? (An obvious tip of the hat to the late Andy Rooney.) An increasingly popular activity – careless use of social media – might very well be the cause of the silent telephone.

The "Social Media" ain't very sociable anymore. The word "social" indicates an interpersonal interaction. It's human contact. People learned about other people by talking and listening, by questioning, and reacting face-to-face in real time. That was the "social" part, and it worked. Yesterday we had handshakes. Today we have icons. Much social interaction now consists of transmitting little bits and pieces of typed information to an unseen audience that includes strangers who are allowed access to what should remain private matters.

Social media in all its various forms are a part of life today, but as with other developments, availability doesn't equal advisability. In fact, it demonstrates the importance of recognizing what has become a very popular label – "unintended consequences." In many respects, that label is a present day version of naive or shortsighted.

Once information enters the social media stream it can travel to unknown destinations, and live forever. That permanency has far-reaching and deep-seated implications for businesses, academia, and applicants.

With increasing frequency, the "first-cut" in processing employment or academic applications is checking the social media entries of an individual. What an applicant voluntarily entered for fun in moments of casualness can suddenly become an obstacle to getting a job – or being admitted to an academic institution. The unfortunate applicant may never know the prospective employer or admissions counselor made the "no-interview" decision based on an old, outdated entry. What the applicant reveals about himself or herself, however, might become extremely important to the reviewer. That may not be "fair," but that's how the system works.

There is no question the variety of social media venues available today have been a boon to businesses by providing advertising opportunities unheard of just a decade ago. Instantaneous and international communication can make any business a global enterprise, but that same global reach can deliver personal information to places it was never intended to go. Today, many people, particularly young people in the pre-teen, teen, and Millennial years are flooding the social media channels with personal information because it's fun to share ideas - and images.

But the "fun" is often distorted by deception, exaggeration, and plain old-fashioned lies. And, as years pass, people who can, and do, make decisions that affect the careers and lives of the unsuspecting participants review the information. Ample data show that most social media users deliberately distort some of what they enter. They describe themselves as bigger, smaller, younger, or older than they really are; they finesse their athletic or artistic ability; they even contribute pictures of themselves that should be kept personal and private. Eventually, the truth appears. What seemed funny at a party can be a disqualifier in the Human Resources or Admissions Office.

It's not only the young ones who engage in the exaggeration and distortion. Parents and other adults share the responsibility.

A recent study showed that 82% of parents knew their children had media accounts when they were underage, and 76% of them actually assisted their underage children in creating accounts. And then, after establishing the account most parents don't monitor the communications. Talk about enabling!

The take-away from all of this is simple. Recognize the power of Social Media, but respect its reach and its life span. Being "too" connected today may be calamitous in the near future. It's important for all of us to think of the long-term implications of our messages before we send them. The sad part about the negative effects of social media is the fact that the victims are the contributors.

Don't be a victim. Don't risk missing out on that interview.

Tale of Two Generations

I wrote this segment on June 6, 2013, the 69th anniversary of the Normandy Invasion. D-Day was one of, if not the greatest, military actions in history. The planning and the ultimate sacrifice of tens of thousands of troops marked a significant turning point in World War II.

The personnel involved, in their mid to late twenties, did what they had to do, and didn't look for praise or thanks or congratulations. I'm sure there was plenty of complaining and "griping," but they did it because it was their job.

Coincidently, on that same day, I read a business report on the intricacies of managing today's workforce which is comprised of four – soon to be five – generations. Of particular note was the realization that the age of the members of Generation X and Y is approximately the same as the troops at Normandy. According to the article, the general characteristic attributed to Gen X and Gen Y, defined as the "Praise Junkies," is the expectation of receiving compliments. In fact, managers were prompted to say a "Compliment Deficit" exists "if employees don't receive a sufficient amount of praise."

As part of what is called a "praise parade" some executives are now using – even requiring – managers to send "Appreciation Notes" to all employees on a regular basis. Such a mandate requires managers to constantly look for items to compliment in order to then be complimented by their own managers. A productive use of time?

Other managers are mandating using "S.A.Y. Notes" which are sent from peer to peer to help everyone feel good. That abbreviation, by the way, stands for "Someone Appreciates You." For anyone needing assistance, a free website displays examples of the notes so no one has to be creative with the compliments much less sincere.

When such communications are required and consist of "stock footage," one wonders what good they do. Hard to see how or why that would be part of the official operation of any organization! Many observers find it difficult to compare the behaviors of the "Narcissist Generation" now in the workforce with those of the "Greatest Generation" when they entered Normandy.

They question if it's even realistic to expect all the different generations to work together in harmony. The answer is, "Yes, it is, and they must!" And that requires all the current generations, and those yet to come in "Generation Z" and beyond to recognize the complexity of the business environment.

Company personnel are commenting that many young applicants manifest what the Mayo Clinic defines as NPD, Narcissistic Personality Disorder, in which people have an "inflated sense of importance and a deep need for admiration believing they are special and acting accordingly."

But it does no good for one generation to point an accusing finger at another, and it's important for the "seasoned members" to recognize that the "newbies" are different. Both parties must acknowledge the value of the comment from Jean Twenge and Keith Campbell in their book, *The Narcissist Epidemic: living in the age of entitlement*, where they wrote, "There is no app for experience."

The take-away in all of this is the appreciation, importance, and application of a basic tenant of effective communication: "Know your audience." Construct and deliver messages that are appropriate and meaningful to the people you are addressing. Focus on what makes them tick, not on just what feels good to you. Recognize that the behaviors of one generation are no better or worse than the behaviors of another. They're just different!

To use a sport analogy: Football and baseball are both great games, but they function under very different sets of rules. And no matter how good you may be, you can't play quarterback on a baseball team. So, as a manager, identify the sport, learn the rules, develop the game plan, know the players, and be willing to make adjustments. Those troops at Normandy did that. And it worked.

We can all learn from their example.

Chapter 12

Just For Fun

You've seen that most of the items included in this book have a rather serious side. That's intended, but everything we encounter during the day isn't serious. Some things are just funny – sometimes outrageous – and we should welcome them and celebrate their existence.

The items in this section fit that definition. They're funny, but they all relate to serious issues.

Enjoy the stories and the situations.

Wheels on a Suitcase or Wings on a Locomotive

During the past few months I've been working with corporate groups interested in using a variety of problem solving techniques.

We've been focusing on Creative Problem Solving,

to be more specific, as opposed to the traditional or analytical problem solving techniques familiar to all of us. The business world has changed and the rate of change is accelerating rapidly. New pressures make it necessary for us to change the way we do business, but old habits often get in the way of new ideas and progress. We tend to stay in our comfort zone rather than exploring new options.

Before going too far, let me explain the title, "Wheels on a suitcase or wings on a locomotive."

Many of us in business don't like to admit we have problems, but I think we would all agree there are plenty of opportunities for improvement if we are flexible and look hard enough. Think about looking at problems from new perspectives.

Wheels on a suitcase is an example of creative problem solving. We have all struggled carrying heave suitcases around airports, but one day someone invented the little wheeled carrier, which allowed us to strap the suitcase on to a compact cart. It was easier walking around, but now we had two items to attend to, the "wheeley" and the suitcase.

Then someone came up with what now seems like an obvious solution. Incorporate the wheels into the structure of the suitcase, and an entirely new device was available.

In the past, suitcases never had wheels, were never intended to have wheels, but now almost every new suitcase you see, large and small alike, has built-in wheels. That was a great idea, and whoever holds the patent is probably very wealthy because of that simple idea.

Here's another example of creative problem solving at work. Think about the space program. Once President John F. Kennedy decreed the US would put a man on the moon within a decade, new ideas and new approaches had to be developed to meet the challenges of space travel. An entirely industry was born, and new technology was developed to achieve the President's lofty goal.

Here's the second part of the title. If engineers had continued to use traditional problem solving techniques of the past they would not have produced the modern spacecraft. If the NASA engineers had used traditional techniques, they would have put wings on a locomotive in order to have a powerful machine that would fly to the moon.

The locomotive is certainly powerful, and wings are necessary for flight so putting them together would be a logical solution to the challenge. Logical, yes, but it wouldn't work. New perspectives resulted in new solutions.

Take a good look around your company, and make a strong effort to see what might be improved. Don't just *look. See* what's there. There's a big difference between "looking" and "seeing."

If you find a problem or an opportunity that should be addressed think about how to get started. When you get an inkling of a product, a service, or a function that might be improved, get out a piece of paper and write down as many questions as you can about it.

Ask, what, why, who, when, how often, should, can, who, if, where, etc., etc. Write them as fast as possible. Then explore solutions from a new point of view. This is an excellent discipline, and it's a good way to keep track of future progress.

Often we hear, "Think outside the box." This is a way to do just that. When we do get out of the box, and we let our ideas soar, interesting results will present themselves.

We might even develop our own business version of a spacecraft rather than putting wings on a corporate locomotive.

Is This The Best You Can Do?

During a seminar I conduct regularly, a participant told an interesting anecdote that has clear implications for many of us. Here is the story. I've since heard other attributions, but we'll stay with this one.

An aide to President Theodore Roosevelt gave him a speech he had been assigned to write. An hour later the president called the aide into his office, held up the speech, and asked, "Is this the best you can do?"

The surprised aide hesitated for a moment and said, "Well, sir, there are probably a few points I could make a little clearer."

"Fine," said the president, and he handed the speech back to the aide who left the room to do a rewrite.

A while later the aide returned with the new draft, and the president thanked him for the quick turn-around. Another hour passed, and the president once again called the aide to the office. He looked the aide right in the eye and once again asked, "Is this the best you can do?"

"I think so, sir." He hesitated again and then said, "But maybe I should take another look to be sure everything is clear. There may still be a couple of items I could make a little tighter." The aide left the office with the second draft.

A short time later the aide returned again with his third draft and handed it to the President. Once again, President Roosevelt asked, "Is this the best you can do?"

This time the aide said, "Yes, sir. This is exactly what you want. I'm sure this is now an excellent speech. One you'll be comfortable delivering"

"Good," said the president. "Now I'll read it."

The aide's first reaction – which he didn't share with the president – was annoyance. The president hadn't even read the first two drafts.

Then the aide realized what the president had done. Without taking any of his time to read the first two drafts, he simply asked a question. The aide evaluated his own work, knew it could be better, and improved it. Mr. Roosevelt never evaluated the first two drafts. He hadn't even read them. He just asked a simple question. The aide did the evaluating, saw it could be better, and revised it twice.

The third version was what the first version should have been before he gave it to the president to read. The aide knew all the time he could do a better job writing the speech, but for reasons known only to him, he didn't take the time or expend the effort to do his best work on the first two drafts.

But he expected the president to use his time to read mediocre material. That's almost insulting to the president. The aide's thinking demonstrated an attitude which said, "I didn't take enough of my time to do this well – twice – but I expect you to use your time to read through it. Sooner or later I'll give you something you'll accept. Then we'll both be happy."

After writing the third draft the aide knew his work was now very good. He finally did what he knew all along he was capable of doing. At the start, however, he tried to get by with inferior work. The lesson here is clear for all of us.

There are probably many instances where we have done work which represented less than our best effort and hoped it would be good enough to get by. We knew we could do better, but for some reason we didn't do any better until we were challenged. The aide in the story finally challenged himself, and he rose to his own expectations.

Regardless of the tasks and opportunities we face, it's probably a good idea for all of us to ask ourselves that same question, "Is this the best I can do?"

Only when we can honestly answer, "Yes. It is." is our job finished.

It's a good question, and a great discipline. Try it.

Business Decisions Often Come First.
The Day Of Two Noons

Since time affects all of us, I thought I'd revisit something I discovered a few years ago about time and how it is designated across the country.

We often hear references to doing business 24/7. The Internet has made that possible, but we must be aware of local times when connecting with clients. My guess is that most business people give little, if any, thought to the genesis of Time Zones.

A logical assumption is that the Federal government developed the concept. However, like many other logical assumptions, that one is incorrect. The four time zones in the US came from business – specifically the US Railroad industry.

As is often the case, the Federal government followed a business decision in adopting the Time Zone designations.

Business days begin and end at approximately the same local times, but because the country includes four time zones, when we plan to make contact with clients and customers it's necessary for us to check not only a clock but also a map. It's easy to find the correct local time in the U.S. because of the clear designation of the boundaries of the time zones, but it wasn't always that way!

I learned about the business contribution years ago when I was walking in downtown Chicago. On the corner of LaSalle and Jackson, I discovered a plaque that describes how the U.S. time zones came into existence. The following text is inscribed on that plaque.

Standard Time System in the United States was adopted on this site on October 11, 1883.

Chicago's famous Grand Pacific Hotel, then on the site of the present Continental Bank building, was the location of the General Time Zone Convention of 1883 which, on October 11 of that year, adopted the current Standard Time System in the United States.

The Convention was called by the nation's railroads. Delegates were asked to develop a better and more uniform time system to govern railroad operations. Previously, time had been determined by the position of the sun with high noon the only existing standard of exact local time.

More than 100 different local times resulted from this method. The new plan proposed by William F. Allen, convention secretary, established four equal time zones across the country. Each one hour ahead of the zone to its west.

All railroad clocks in each zone were to be synchronized to strike the hour simultaneously. The Standard Time System was inaugurated on November 18, 1883. On that day, known as the "Day of Two Noons," the Allegheny observatory at the University of Pennsylvania transmitted a telegraph signal when it was exactly noon on the 90th meridian. Railroad clocks throughout the U.S. were then reset on the hour according to the time zone.

Although implemented by the railroads, the

Federal government, states, and cities began to
use the system almost immediately. On March
19, 1918, Congress formally acknowledged the
plan by passing the Standard Time Act.

This plaque is presented to the Continental
Bank by the Midwest Historical Society, Inc. on
November 18, 1971.

Not only was this a significant historical fact, but it
also demonstrated another valuable contribution a group
of businessmen made to the country. Thirty-five years
passed before Congress formalized the decision the railroad executives made at that meeting. The Time Zone
designation made at the Convention was good for the
railroad business, but it was also good for the country.

We've all seen those time zone lines zig-zagging
down our maps. Now we know who put them there. If
you have the time and the inclination, look at the plaques
you pass on your travels.

But don't just look at them, read them. You might
discover something interesting.

About the Author

Bob Parkinson has served as a communications consultant and coach for numerous Fortune 500 companies working successfully at all levels of corporate, government, and academic institutions from CEO's to new hires. In addition, he has taught more than 1750 communication related programs for clients in the U.S. and internationally and consulted and conducted research in South America, Africa, and Australia.

He earned a Ph.D. degree from Syracuse University. His other degrees are: MA in Management and Supervision, and BA in English and Biology from Montclair State University (NJ).

After serving on active duty in the U.S. Army, Parkinson began his professional career as a high school teacher. Subsequent professional positions include Faculty, Northwestern University; Associate Dean, National Louis University; Director of Research, Office of the Governor, Il; Director of Research, Bell & Howell.

He lives with his wife, Eileen, in Sarasota, Florida.

www.ingramcontent.com/pod-product-compliance
Lightning Source LLC
Chambersburg PA
CBHW071956040426
42447CB00009B/1351